Vijay Tendulkar: As a Feminist Playwright

Dr.Manohar.A.Wasnik

INDIA • SINGAPORE • MALAYSIA

ISBN 979-8-89610-262-5

“Her wings are cut and then she is blamed for not knowing how to fly”

Simon de Beauvoir, The Second Sex

Dedicated to my Baba and Aai

who went out of the window,

but they planted the seed of knowledge in my mind,

nurtured it,

and made me capable for shining a star.

Contents

Foreword

One of the most significant playwrights in India, Vijay Tendulkar, is recognized as a feminist voice in contemporary Indian theatre. He tackled the intricate societal problems of gender, power, and patriarchy in his works. His plays, such as "Silence! The Court is in Session", "Sakharam Binder", and "Kamala", questioned the traditional roles that are allocated to women in Indian society and critically analysed the subjugation of women there. Tendulkar frequently places his female characters in oppressive settings, reflecting broader feminist issues via their fights for dignity and autonomy. His audacious stories subverted social mores, establishing him as a progressive voice in support of gender equality.

The corpus of work produced by Vijay Tendulkar is a potent tribute to his keen awareness of the underlying conflicts and undercurrents in society. His plays have left a lasting impression on the Indian theatre because of their deep emotionality, unwavering realism, and courageous exploration of human behaviour.

We examine the harsh truths of human existence as they are portrayed in three of Vijay Tendulkar's foundational works such as "Silence! The Court is in Session", "Sakharam Binder", and "Kamala". These plays are mirrors held up to the faces of individuals who dare to look closely at society's moral framework, its hypocrisies, and its power systems rather than just theatrical productions. Tendulkar's brilliance resides in his capacity to humanise intricate social issues without lessening their seriousness. Despite being audacious, multifaceted, and frequently incredibly defective, his characters inspire compassion and reflection. Tendulkar uses a pretend trial in "Silence! The Court is in Session" to critically examine how society treats women, which gradually turns into a harsh exercise of patriarchal dominance. The drama portrays the subtle discrimination that women experience in a society that is meant to be progressive through the character of LeelaBenare, the heroine.

In the play "Sakharam Binder", the author delves deeply into the life of a man who opposes traditional morals, only to find himself caught in the exact society standards he so shamelessly refuses. This confrontation with raw and unfiltered reality leaves the spectator speechless.

Conversely, the play "Kamala" reveals the transactional aspect of interpersonal interactions, particularly in a world controlled by men where women are practically traded off. It forces us to consider the monetization of women and the ethical void that even highly educated men experience, challenging our moral comfort zones.

The plays of Tendulkar are not restricted by location, time, or cultural background. They still have important things to say about freedom, power, morality, and human suffering. His distinct theatrical style is distinguished by his dramatic devices, which include his ability to push social boundaries, his skilful use of dialogue, and his blurring of the borders between absurdity and realism. The reader will be drawn into Tendulkar's complex, multi-layered, and frequently terrifying universe within these pages.

Every play serves as an invitation to consider one's own involvement in the systems of power, to question social standards, and to face difficult facts. This book is a celebration of Tendulkar's artistic vision and his great comprehension of human nature rather than merely an examination of his work. Vijay Tendulkar questioned not only the rules of theatre but also the conscience of a society that is averse to acknowledging its own flaws through his writing. We are reminded that excellent theatre goes beyond just amusement as we explore in the plays - *Silence! The Court is in Session, Sakharam Binder, and Kamala.* It makes people think, feel, and, most importantly, want things to change.

I congratulate Dr.ManoharWasnik for making this successful effort to bring out crucial aspects of the literary creed of Vijay Tendulkar's plays. This book will provide an in-depth critique on all the three plays taken up here for interpretation.

I invite students, scholars, researchers, and teachers to read this book **"Vijay Tendulkar: As a Feminist Playwright"** to understand Vijay Tendulkar as a playwright and the various aspects and dimensions of his literary creations with special focus on feminism.

Dr.Vitthal Gore
Head, Department of English,
ShriHavagiswami College, Udgir,
Dist. Latur, Maharashtra, India.
17 September 2024.

Preface

Dear Academicians/ Researchers/Readers,

Welcome to "Vijay Tendulkar: As a Feminist Playwright." The present book sharpens minds of fondling drama and understands the approach towards feminism. As the author of the present book, I firmly believe this book helps to understand the vision and mission of Vijay Tendulkar as a feminist playwright. He himself denied being a feminist, but his several plays build a platform where women not only expose the darkness of their suffering and exploitation but also show the outlet of liberation for themselves.

Here the author specially focused on three plays: *Silence! The Court is in Sessions Sakharam Binder and Kamala,* in which we strongly realize that the playwright approaches towards half of the population of India that remains aloof from the mainstream of the progress. It is a comprehensive and profound effort to unravel the various aspects and elements of feminism that are hidden in the plays of veteran playwright Vijay Tendulkar. The book deals with women who are puppets in the hands of men and face a lot of challenges. They suffer, and their journey of exploitation finds a ray of hope for liberation. Try to find liberation from all kinds of tragic resonance.

The present book is divided into seven chapters. Chapter one, entitled "Introduction," is a critical analysis of feminism and exposes various definitions. It also puts forth a history of feminism. Chapter two, "The Dramatic World of Vijay Tendulkar," demonstrates Vijay Tendulkar's personal and dramatic world. For him, writing is a passion that brings relief and joy, and therefore, on each and every occasion, he utilizes it to expose human experiences through writing. He considers writing an independent mental activity used for pleasure or professional gain. As a responsible writer, he admits that his role as a playwright comes afterwards. Tendulkar adopts the method of 'trial and error' to sharp dramatic structure and technique.

The chapter third, entitled "Vijay Tendulkar as a Feminist," truly reveals the journey of a feminist writer. Though Vijay Tendulkar himself denied being a feminist writer, the author attempts to prove Tendulkar as a feminist writer by interpreting and scrutinizing three plays. Here deals with various aspects and elements of feminism, which are discovered in three plays.Tendulkar has become an important spokesperson for the downtrodden, weak and exploited masses, including the women. Many of his plays present the position of women in the contemporary modern society

The chapter forth, entitled "Silence! The Court is in Session: Patriarchal Society and Exploitation," unravels an important aspect of feminism. The character Leela Benare in Silence is an intellectual woman. She retains her femininity and her inner strength to challenge the force of patriarchal exploitation, but her boldness and cheerfulness are destroyed by patriarchal society and culture. Here, the author focuses on the impact of patriarchal culture on Leela Benare's life. At the beginning of the play, she flies like a free bird, but in the course of the play, the male-dominated society grips her in the net and cuts her wings.

Fifth chapters, so-called "Kamala: The Liberation of Woman, "show the life journey of three women, Sarita, Kamala, and Kamalbai, in male-dominated society. Vijay Tendulkar projects all three women on the basis of realism. They are plunged under the pressure of patriarchy. Jaisingh Jadhav exploits all three women and makes the utmost use of their lives to gain position and reputation in the family and society. His policy of 'use and throw' regarding Kamala is the obvious and uppermost peak of his hypocrisy. As mentioned, the sufferers of his hypocrisy are three different women belonging to three different strata of society. Kamala is the lowest in the order, hence is the most oppressed one. Similarly, Kamalabai too belongs to the lower strata, and her poverty makes her helpless.

"Sakharam Binder: The Conflict between Powerful and Powerless" sixth chapter explores the conflict between the mighty power of Sakharam Binder and powerless women Laxmi and Champa. We witness the conflict among the three characters. The presence of both women, Laxmi and Champa, creates chaos and conflict in Sakharam's life. Before the entry of Champ in the house of Sakharam, he uses male power over Laxmi. It shows a complex psychological effect on him. Sakharam intends to fulfil his desires by suppressing two women. As a consequence, the conflict takes place among three and transforms into the murder of Champa. On one hand, Sakharam is dissatisfied with Laxmi's coolness and religiosity, and on the other hand, Champa's powerful body makes Sakharam powerless. The last chapter is conclusion and covers and summarizes all chapters and the final estimation of Vijay Tendulkar as a feminist playwright.

I am very delighted to present this book. The journey of drama is a profound exploration of human emotions, thoughts and philosophy. It is my faith that it will help readers and researchers to understand ideas, thoughts skill of Vijay Tendulkar about writing plays and his approach towards women.

Acknowledgment

Publication of this book would not have been possible without the assistance of many people. I am sincerely indebted to. Dr.Vithal Gore, Head, Department of English,Shri Havagiswami College, Udgir, Dist. Latur. (M.S.) He has given foreword and taken great efforts to clarify some the ideas about the book. I really acknowledge all his worthy contributions of time, ideas and precious guidance to make this productive and thought- provoking book.

I am sincerely thankful to. Dr.Amol Raut, Head, Department of English, Yashoda Girls' Arts and Commerce College, Nagpur. (M.S.) There are three plays of Vijay Tendulkar which are very intricate to understand but the guidance of Dr.Amol Raut has helped me to overcome all the difficulties. His inspiration, constant and constructive advice encouraged me to complete the book.

I would like to express my gratitude to Dr. M. R. Ingle, retired professor and head, Department of Commerce, Shri Shivaji College, Akola. Prof. Rupesh Rele, Vasntrao Kolhatkar Arts College Rohana, R.A. College Washim Dr. Dinesh Ingle, Shivaji College, Akola Dr. Pravin Waghmare for being a vital force of support behind me.

I am also thankful to Dr. Sanjay Patil, Principal of Sahakar Maharshi Late Bhaskarrao Shingne Arts College Khamgon. I am very happy to mention the names of my colleagues, Dr. H.P. Yeole and Dr. N.D. Deshmukh. Dr. P.R. Chavan, Dr. D.U. Raut, Dr. G.S.Vishwakarma, and Mr.G.S. Rakhonde for their motivation. I am also thankful to S.A. Lande, Liberian, who issued me books anytime.

I would like to thank my all close friends Prof. Rahul Mahure, S.P.M. College, Nadura, Prof. Prakash Gawai, L.R.T. College, L.R.T.College,Akola, Dr.Rajendra Waghnmare, and S.R. Mohata.

College, Khamgaon, Nituraj Gawai, and Prof Akash Haral, Shri Shivaji College, Akola, for their love and support.

I convey my gratitude from the core of my heart to the biggest source of my strength, my family and relatives. I wish to convey my sincere thanks to my sisters, brothers, father-in-- law, mother-in-law, and brother-in-law for their ever blessings and best wishes and persuading me for the value of sincerity and consistent cooperation about my academic venture. I don't have words that express the assistance and helping nature of my better half, Amrapali, in the course of the book. I extend the special thanks to my active daughters, Sarthi and Kimaya, who have allowed me to take the time from her required company.

I express my humble gratitude to Notion Press, which makes available to me a platform for publishing this book and provides acknowledgement worldwide recognition as an author.

I also express my sincere gratitude to the principal, Dr. Sudhir Chavan, because of whose support I could complete this work. I thank the following people for helpful discussions with them: Dr. D.T. Adhau, G.S. College, Kamgaon, Dr. Sanjay Vitte, R.D.G. College, Akola, Dr. Dipak Wankhade, Shri Shivaji College, Akola, and Dr. A.R. Ingle. Shri Shivaji College, Akot. I also thank those who have directly or indirectly supported me to complete this book.

Dr.Manohar Wasnik

ACRONYMS

Plays

* STCIS: Silence! The Court is in Session

*KML: Kamala

* SKB :Sakharam Binder

* KND :Kanyadan

1 Introduction

The term 'feminism' originated from the Latin word 'Femina' meaning 'woman'. It was first used in the context of equality and the Women's Rights Movement. The word 'female' signifies something deficient in female', which suggests that women are inferior to the male. The Greek philosopher Aristotle also states similar views about sex: "The male is by nature superior and the female inferior, the male ruler and the female subject. Males enjoy supremacy in every walk of life, while females are deprived of rights" (Smith). They have been considered physically, intellectually, mentally, and emotionally weaker than men, and such considerations give them a subordinate or lower status in every sphere of life.

Feminism is an ideology that aims at protecting the political, legal, economic and social restrictions on the fundamental rights of women which have existed throughout history and all civilizations. The justification of equality and providing rights to women is the sole purpose of feminism. Many critics, feminists, thinkers, philosophers, advocates of equality between man and woman and attempt to define feminism in different ways and on different issues. One such critic of feminism, Karen Offen defines, "a concept that can encompass both an ideology and a movement for socio-political change based on critical analysis of male privilege and women's subordination within any given society"(82).

In general, feminism implies a way of life that fights against such discriminative concepts of masculine and feminine. It aims at creating outlook and perception towards suppression, oppression among women. However, feminism is an umbrella notion and it needs to be understood in its wider sense as it refers to the consciousness of identity as a woman and concerns in feminine problems. Its connotation should not be confined to the mere advocacy of women's rights. Feminism has become an international school. There are different schools like Liberal, Marxist, Socialist, Existentialist, and Postmodern, etc schools of feminism. Aiming at women's liberty, these modern theories cover diverse aspect of life. They interpret women's life in various ways and discover causes of women's suffering and subjugation in the world.

Feminism strongly asserts in equal social and political rights to women to those possess by men. It is a movement to acquire such rights made by a male in the presence of feminine characteristics.Throughout centuries women have been struggling to liberate themselves from male domination and oppression. Obviously, the aim of feminism has been articulated long ago. Inequalities, injustices, oppression of women are prime issues of feminism.

There is a variety of views and strong differences among feminists and critics regarding the nature of justice and injustice. The well known feminist journalist, Rebecca West remarks that "I myself have never been able to find out precisely what "Feminism" is; I only know that people call me a feminist whenever I express sentiments that differentiate me from a doormat or a prostitute"(119). This simple view of the West towards feminism suggests that it has been defined from person to person.

Simone de Beauvoir, the ardent feminist and philosopher who was influenced by existentialism. She clarifies that "One is not born, but rather becomes a woman. No biological, psychological or economic fate determines the figure that the human female presents in society; it is civilization as a whole that produces this creature, intermediate between male and eunuch, which is described as feminine"(301). The illustration from Beauvoir clearly demonstrates that it is the whole civilization that provides the mark for a woman as a woman and the same proves the root cause of women's oppression.

In her well-known book *The Second Sex*, Beauvoir writes that "the woman is defined and differentiated with reference to man and not he with reference to her; she is the incidental, the inessential as opposed to the essential. He is the Subject; he is the Absolute, she is the other" (16). In relation to men, women have been relegated to a secondary position since ancient time. The feminine feature of a woman is neglected to define her being. Men control social tradition and customs so that men define a woman with their own interests.

The conviction of feminism is that women are oppressed or disadvantaged by comparison with men and their oppression becomes in some way illegitimate or unjustified. Other post-modern feminists Alice Jardine states that "who and what, then do we mean by "feminist"? That word...poses some serious problems. Not that we would want to end up demanding a definition of what feminism is, and therefore, of what one must do, say, and be if one is to acquire the epithet; dictionary meanings are suffocating, to say the least" (20). Jardine seems very critical of dictionary meanings of the term; instead, she would have it as the epithet for "the second sex".

We can simply recognize from the above discussion that the central or main issue of feminism seems to be the recognition of marginalization of women, male dominance, the existence of inequality, and sexual discrimination. The theory and its practitioners are stoutly committed to representing women; allotting meaning and creating a social space for them are the basic features of this movement. In short, the concept cannot be assigned any particular definition as it strives to re-establish the identity of the woman as an individual, not merely the'second sex'.

Feminists are trying to develop a theory, social practice in the following ways. First, they demand that there should not be a sexual division of labour in the workplace and in political organizations of all ideological persuasions and second it believes in a differentiated social order within which various dimensions are distinct but not separate or opposed.

Broadly speaking, feminism is a phenomenon of social change. It attempts to liberate women from the manacles and constraints of a male-dominated society and facilitates them to enjoy their rights as free human beings. It intends to rebel against an adverse situation in which a woman is compelled to live. The main objective of feminism is to improve the status of women and provide equal opportunity and dignity with men. Feminism aims at compulsory education for women and improves the employability for women. The writers or people, who are influenced by the feminist thought or idea, involved themselves in expressing their ideas in their actions, social reformation, and literary writings, which has led to the development of feminist literature.

After understanding the concept and views of the theorist and feminist, it is important to study feminism in the Indian context. Indian feminism has a different scenario. It has a long history of the suffering of women, the bitter struggle on behalf of women's rights, and gender inequality that has persisted. Indian society has always been highly hierarchical. The several hierarchies function within the family unit itself; associated with age, sex, etc. The other hierarchies also operate in friendly relationships or within the community, with hierarchy referring to the caste lineage, learning, occupation, etc. All such hierarchies have been followed very strictly and have caused fragmentation, division, and discrimination in human beings. Suma Chitnis describes the reaction to the feminist movement in India:

> The most distinctive feature of this movement is that it was initiated by man. It was only towards the end of the century the women joined the fray. The list of who, champion the cause of women is long –Raja Ram Manohar Roy, Ishwarchandra Vidya Sagar, Keshav Chandra Sen, Matahari, Phule, Agarkar, Ranade, Karve to mention a few. The record of the reform they undertook to achieve is impressive. It reveals that their efforts spanned action to abolish the practice of Sati, the custom of child marriage, a custom of distinguishing widows, the ban on remarriage of the upper caste Hindu widows and many other civil practices that affected women. (VII)

It is surprising to know that the Western feminist movement was initiated by women whereas in India men took efforts in the direction and women joined later. During the 19th-century women's issues come under the highlight and reforms began to be made. Until the end of the Nineteenth century, the status of women was dreadful like that of domestic animal. When the British came to India, the condition of the women was at the worst. The social reformers like Raja Ram Mohan Roy, Maharshi Karve, Ishwar Chandra Vidya Sagar, Vishnushastri Pandit, etc started social reform movements.

Having understood the wretched condition of women, they strongly advocated for the education of women. A new awareness created the voice of women's subordination. Though English education had been introduced, it was limited only a few families. They educated their girls either at school or at home. The traditional social barriers were so strong and it was impossible to break them easily. The evils like child marriage, widowhood, Sati and woman subservience still clutched the society. The early Indian writers expressed their thoughts in English, reflecting the existing social ambivalence in their works. They had to balance their newly acquired western thoughts with the existing social scenario.

As far as Maharashtra state is concerned, the movement was started independently a little later. Savitri Bai Phule, Tarabai Shinde, and Pandita Ramabai were great feminists. Savitri Bai Phule started the first school for girls in India along with her husband, Jotibha Phule. Pandita Ramabai strongly assaulted patriarchy and the caste system. She was a rebel who married outside her caste and converted to Christianity. Tarabai Shinde wrote India's first feminist text. The tradition of 'Sati' was a dirty stain on Indian society, so Bengali reformers have given their significant contribution in abolishing 'Sati'. It was a horrible custom in which people used to burn a widow alive on her husband's funeral pyre. They also strove to eradicate the custom of child marriage and introduced the remarriage of upper-caste Hindu widows.

Comparatively, the Indian women writers could not express their thoughts and ideas liberally as the western women writers could. They did so in a cautious manner, avoiding any resistance and controversy with orthodox people and traditionalists. Malashri Lai observes the following about these works:

> Romantic attachments that she read in Charlotte Bronte or George Eliot were immensely alluring to the intellect but totally false to her own position as an object agreeable to an arranged marriage. Through flights of fancy, the womanwriter could transform some of her insistent reality. What she managed in these transformations was re-telling of her own life in one way or the other. (5)

However, the beginning of the twentieth century was enthusiastic; the literate middle-class women participated in the nationalist movement.

Women's liberation was also a part of this movement. Many organizations of women and movements came forward. Mahatma Gandhi took initiatives to encourage women. He also invited the women as a class to participate on a massive scale in the 'The movement of freedom struggle'. He started ones a civil disobedience movement in 1930. Jawaharlal Nehru mentioned in his book *Discovery of India:*

> Most of us men folk were in prison. And then a remarkable thing happened. Our women came to the front and took charge of the struggle. Women had always been there, of course, but now there was an avalanche of them, which took not only the British Government but their own men folk by surprise. Here were these women, women of the upper or middle classes, leading sheltered lives in their homes - peasant women, working-class women, rich women -pouring out in their tens of thousands in defiance of government order.It was not only that display of courage and daring but what was even more surprising was the organizational power they showed. (41)

In modern India, the position of woman has changed considerably. Her status in modern Indian society is equal to that of men, socially, economically, educationally, politically and legally. Now, she has equal rights to receive education, inherit own property, participate in public life and political life of the nation. Like the man, she has become economically independent. She has come forth out of the domestic constraints. She can seek employment anywhere. Therefore, she is certainly enjoying equal status with man in all fields of life. There are so many factors responsible to bring out the change in women's condition like women's education; reform movements by many social reformers, women participation in politics and much social legislation

Education plays a vital role in women's lives. It is the most effective index of development. In the past, women were confined to the four walls of the house. But education broke the limitations of women and gave them entry into the new world. Since the Industrial Revolution in Europe, there has been a gradual change in the world economy and especially in the outlook of women. After World War II, there were more and more devastations, reconstructions, technological advancements, scientific discoveries, and changes in the family system, ethical, moral, spiritual values, and so on.

The second half of the 20th century brought out the change, and women have appeared in all fields and all walks of life. It is undoubtedly education that has emancipated women from within the four walls of the home. But the position or status, the restrictions on their role in society, the level of empowerment, the level of gender sensitivity, the gender stereotypes, and the amount of emancipation due to modernization differ from country to country, from state to state, from region to region, and from one religious group to another that leads to problems of varied dimensions.

The establishment of independent women's organizations gained greater self-determination for the second sex in the 20th century. A new storyline began to be constructed regarding women's activism by the late thirties and forties. This was newly explored and bolstered with the perception to create a 'logical' and organic relationship between feminism and Marxism, as well as with anti-communalism and anti-casteism, etc. Dr. Ambedkar was a great follower of humanity and incorporated the values of liberty, equality, and fraternity in the Indian Constitution. The Constitution of India guaranteed 'equality between the sexes,' which provided a relative breather in women's movements until the 1970s.

As compared to Western feminism, Indian feminists have to face certain problems and adversities in India. Indian feminists have the same ultimate goal as their Western counterparts; their version of feminism can differ in many respects in order to tackle the kind of issues and circumstances they face in the modern-day patriarchal society of India. Mostly Indian feminists strive to challenge the patriarchal structure in several ways. In the field of religion, Indian feminists pay their attention to the powerful image of female goddesses in Hinduism. They also refer to the matriarchal prehistory of Indian society and stress the fact that there have been times in Indian history that the societies were not patriarchal. There existed largely female-oriented and matriarchal societies in the nation.

The diversity of the Indian experience unfolds multiple patriarchies that in turn contribute to the existence of multiple feminisms. Hence, feminism is not a singular theoretical orientation in India. It has revolutionized over time in relation to historical and cultural realities. As a result, women have changed their levels of consciousness, perceptions, and actions of individual women, and women as a group. The patriarchal society began acknowledging sexism. Feminists are attempting to eliminate the system and challenge it through deconstructing mutually exclusive concepts of femininity and masculinity as biologically determined categories.

In the post-Independence era, the Indian feminist activists are squashed between traditional Marxism and radical feminism. Thus the third accepted form was liberal feminism. They were contributed by the Western school of thought. As far as the Indian women's movement is concerned, these three forms do have a very significant impact.

Marxist theory primarily spotlights on production, exploitation and property. It more emphasises on the removal of economic inequality that exists between the classes. They consider that it is the only solution to establish equality. Thus, it is the wide chasm that exists between the haves and have-nots in Marxism. So it is easy for the oppressed and exploited women to fit into the large canvas of the have-nots.

Kate Millet's *Sexual Politics* was an important book that evolved the Radical Feminists theory. Radical Feminism originated in the late 1960's. It declared men as real enemies of womanhood and women's power. Radical Feminism observes patriarchal society as the main oppressor of women. The weapon used by the family to subjugate women is harassment and violence. Radical Feminists believe that this conflict between the sexes existed in prehistoric times and believe that all the existing principles have succeeded in marginalising women.

Liberal Feminism is another discipline of feminism. It endeavours to create freedom within rather than striving for freedom. It focuses on female space within the existing structure, without the least amount of confrontation. They neglect the question of sexuality by accepting the sex roles as decreed by the Establishment. They question all the other forces that label women as inferior. They emphasise that the civil rights of women, like the right to education, right of expression, and all her civil rights, should be implemented as legality. Liberals feel that a radical restructuring of society will never have the power to withstand the damages of time.

When we study feminism or the new theories of feminism, one thing clearly comes to mind: there is no union between these divergent movements. Though their ways are different, their goal and target are the same: to eradicate the exploitation of women. Radicals work for a complete reformation of society based on gender equality, and the liberals accept the stratification, fight for making women visible in history, and try to retrieve the significant role played by women in creating history. These movements have made a positive contribution to the Indian women. They become aware, though not very intensely, of the exploitation and violence that hinder her all-round progress.

It may be true that feminism in India has been considerably influenced by the thought and feminist movement in the West; still, feminism, as it exists in India, has surpassed its western counterparts. The comment of Uma Nayantara is appropriate here: "third world feminism is not mindless mimicking of western agenda in one clear and simple sense" (243).

The Dramatic World of Vijay Tendulkar

The contemporary Indian drama is versatile and comprehensive. It has been calculated or analyzed in the light of modern approaches like psychoanalytical, feministic, cultural studies, gender studies, archetypal, formalist, post-structuralism, Marxist, etc. However, all the approaches cannot explore every aspect and every fragment. Something remains relatively unexplored. Therefore, the further developments happened in contemporary theory, in critical approaches, recent techniques, and in innovative themes. All new techniques and theories are applied to comprehend the depth of drama. The new theories facilitate the ideas and insights that might unfold its manifold aspects.

Modern Indian drama has achieved a remarkable depth which requires critical scrutiny and analysis. It is relatively and greatly divorced from the philosophical creeds of its predecessors and has come up as an effective medium of expression with the mechanism of power domination, new patterns of personal relationship, and the disintegration of the old values. It is characterized by its modest way to deal with contemporary social issues of its time.

Modern playwrights usually deal with realistic characters and their personal issues in order to address a social problem. During the Twentieth century, Indian drama grew with realism as compared to classical drama. It employs social contemporary issues existing in society. They expose burning issue in their plays.

The pioneers like Mohan Rakesh, Vijay Tendulkar, Badal Sircar, Girish Karnad and Mahesh Dattanibestowed a new identity to Indian drama and set a new direction which becomes an instrument for demonstrating the voice of Indians. These pioneers are credited to devise a strategy for indigenous aesthetics and dramaturgy. Result of their experiments within the drama, they could reinvestigate legends, history, myth, and folklore.

Girish Karand is originally Kannada writer executed the role of the director as well as the actor. The travelling Natak companies influenced him.A leading playwright, eminent master of performingKarandwas honoured with the Jnanpith award. He studied at Oxford and worked as a teacher at the University of Chicago. He left his job and committed himself to playwriting. He wrote his plays in Kannada language and afterward, his plays were translated into English, some of his plays were translated into English by the playwright himself. As a playwright Karnad is well known for his plays: *Yayati*(1961),*Yayati* (1961), *Tughlaq* (1964), *Hayavadana* (1971), *Angumalige* (1974), *HihinaHunja* (1980), *Naga-Mandala* (1988), *Tale Danda* (1990), *Fire and Rain* (1994), *Agni Mattu Male* (1995), *Bali: The Sacrifice* (2004) and *The Wedding Album* (2009). Greatly influenced by German playwright Bertolt Brecht, Karnad deals with existentialist issues like a split personality, identity crisis, ideological break-ups, and division of life in his plays.

The versatile theatre personality, Mahesh Dattani was a drama teacher, stage director, actor, and Bharatnatyam dancer. He is the first Indian dramatist to win the *Sahitya Akademi Award* in 1998. He established a performing arts group "Playpen" in 1984. Dattani holds theatre courses at Portland State University USA. He also writes radio plays for BBC and conducts workshops. Dattani has nine plays to his credit. They are *Where there is A Will* (1986) ,*Dance Like a Man* (1989), *Tara* (1990), *Bravely Fought the Queen* (1991), *Final Solutions* (1992), *Nigh Queen* (1996), *On a Muggy Night in Mumbai* (1998), *Thirty Days in September* (2001). Being the voice of India, Dattani's plays embody many of the classic concern for the world drama. His plays depict religious tension, sexuality and gender issues and characters are taken mostly from the urban middle class.

Another genius Badal Sircar (also known as Badal Sarkar) exposed the existential demeanorof modern life and devised a people's Third Theatre. He also created anti-theatre to highlight the problem of Naxalites. He is well-known for his plays *Solution X, Evam Indrajit, That Other History*

(1964), *There is not End* (1971), *PaglaGhoda, Palapa, Procession, Bhoma,* and *Stale News.*

The post independence period is the combination ofpessimism and optimism. The dark side of the period and feeling of pessimism are found in the dramatic works of Girish Karnad, Mohan Rakesh, Badal Sircar and, Vijay Tendulkar. These four playwrights skilfully expose day- to-day life. Tendulkar plays a crucial role in dramatic world and has been acknowledged as the leading dramatist of the *avant-garde* movement in the Indian context.

Vijay Tendulkar (1928-2008) can be considered as the pioneer of modern Indian English drama. Most of his plays deal with the problems of women and conflict between the individual and society. As a result, the angry and frustrated protagonists of his plays are actually the sufferers of bitter circumstances in their life. Since Tendulkar explores the grim facet of the society, therefore, his plays take birth of controversy in his life. The central idea of his plays is power, violence, and exploitation of women, man-woman relationship, male domination, and denial of social norms. He deeply seeks into the human mind and its complexities in all its depth and diversity. He never represents human relationships in terms of romanticism, love, and emotions but in sensuality and violence. A fearless depiction of reality and interpretative power, artistic gist of Tendulkar have made him one of the most controversial and at the same time, admired of Indian playwrights.

Vijay Tendulkar is probably the first Marathi playwright who has not only brightened the regional theatre but also achieved worldwide fame and reverence by contributing to the world of literature. His plays were translated into English and many other regional languages and staged in other regional and international languages. Although he started writing plays in the 1950s, those early plays were considered as the 'experimental'. Having experimented with all aspects of the play, including content, acting, decor and audience communication like other young playwrights, Tendulkar provided a path to Marathi theatre. Tendulkar has not just contributed to the modern Marathi theatre but has given it a new dimension and a new form.

Vijay Tendulkar accepted and employed the tools and techniques in his early one-act plays that found in contemporary European and American theatre. Tendulkar spent his life in the world that filled up with the exploitation of human beings. Social order was filled with communal violence, political unrest, and the subordinate status of women. Tendulkar's vivid portrayal of the oppression of women evidences his compassion and empathy for women and shows his attachment to feministic outlook. Human sufferings and respect for human beings is the soul of his plays.

Vijay Tendulkar's literary contribution has surpassed in Marathi Literature. His plays may appear to be straightforward and simple on a surface level, but it demands a deep explanation before taking any conclusion. His works reveal different perspectives and raise the controversy on many occasions. At the outsets of his literary career, he had been alleged that he was just animpressionist of the Western dramatic works. Some critics criticized that his plays were translated from other languages which seem to be without a base. Apparently, this may be a fact that his literary works have the western touch, but the same touch or inspiration should not be considered as an imitation or the copy of western dramas. Inspiration is the root cause of his creativity and inspiration never becomes a copy of the copy. T.S. Eliot states that 'historical sense' is obtained by great labor. It involves a perception, not only of the pastness of the past but of its presence. So, on the base of Eliot's definition, the allegations on Vijay Tendulkar seem improper, illogical and incorrect. His dramatic achievement proves the fact that mere imitator cannot produce such qualitative and creative literary work in his life. Arundhati Banerjee rightly confirms, "Vijay Tendulkar has been in the vanguard of not just Marathi but Indian theatre for almost forty years"(vii).

Like Shakespeare, Tendulkar also participated and acted in the plays at his young age. He developed the initial sense of the plays in the surroundings of theater and learned by a trial-and-error method. Similar to Shakespeare, he has also made a huge contribution to Marathi literature by attempting every genre of literature. He has written twenty-eight full-length plays and given his spectacular literary contribution. Other contributions of Vijay Tendulkar are also equally important in Marathi literature and consist of his four collections of short stories, eleven plays for children, one novel, and five volumes of literary essays and social criticism, all of which have contributed to a remarkable renovation of the modern literary landscape of Maharashtra and that of the nation as a whole. So, we can call Tendulkar Marathi Shakespeare. We can realize his deep passion for writing from the following statement when Tendulkar shares his view with Shanta Gokhale:

> Give me a piece of paper, any paper, and a pen, and I shall write as naturally as a bird flies or a fish swims. He has said. For the last forty years, I have been writing sitting in newspaper offices in the roadside restaurants, on the crowded running local trains and when my living space did not allow me to be myself and write, I have written sitting in the bathroom. And I have written in the sick bed in the hospital in the spore of the doctor advised not to tax myself. He did not know and would not accept that writing was not taxing to me at all, on the contrary, it was soothing. It was a great relief. It was a joy. (78-79)

Tendulkar is also a great translator in Marathi. He has translated nine novels,two biographies, and five plays into Marathi. He is known for original stories and screenplays for eight films in Marathi, including *Umbartha* (*The Threshold*) (1981), a milestone feature film based on women's activism in India. In brief, he has touched every genre of literature, but as a playwright, he excelled in his literary career.

The society is a great source of inspiration for an artist. There is no doubt; he may be influenced by society as well as he influences society. The same is applicable to the drama of the west. As far as the Indian scene, liberated trade, industrialization, and urbanization have greatly influenced Indian literature. The new developments created a split in society and separated the classes. The twentieth century, in general, has witnessed the collapse of the old patterns of social life.

Western dramatists like John Osborne and Wesker took up theater for political anger and revolt. Tendulkar was a voracious reader, so he read Marx deeply. He was influenced by Marxist ideas and came forward to protest against exploitation, oppression of women, as well as man-class conflict. Though he was a staunch defender of a non-violent humane path of Buddhism, in spite of the fact that the fact that he exposed the violence in human beings in his plays. Like Karl Marx, he treats him as human beings. To create a social awakening among the mass of the poor and workers, Tendulkar depicts the angry and perturbed protagonists of the contemporary young generation of India. Moreover, his reflection is objective and realistic. He presented a true picture of society. Some of the characters are miserable and pitiable, while others are rough and tough.

Tendulkar has undermined the tradition of a stage and dealt with contemporary issues. As a writer and playwright, Tendulkar has an inherent ability to involve and distance himself from his creation. Humour and intense compassion form the dominant elements of his creation, which sometimes are difficult to perceive owing to their barely visible quality. It bestows infinite delicacy to his work yet none of his creations are ever simplistic.

His dramatic world begins with the writing of one-act plays; *The House Holder* and subsequently *The Rich*. However, these plays have the traditional dramatic structure and reveal the individuality of the writer, novelty in subject matter and treatment. His earlier plays like *The House Holder*, *An Island Called Man*, and *The Middle Walls* exposed his inclination towards the complexities of middle-class life. The audience grasps the story of his middle-class man as well as feels the complexity of the middle-class mentality and behaviour. His characters are simple and coarse persons that one would meet in the ordinary world.

Tendulkar artistically exposes simple and straightforward people who turn violent, who love, hate and envy each other; women enslaved by men, compelled by circumstances, lonely and alienated men and so on. Ramakant in *An Island Called Man* and Rama in *The Vultures* can be cited as illustrative examples. Through the personal relationships of his characters Tendulkar explorers the theme of man's existential loneliness and exploitation of women.

The first period of his literary career is illuminated with the plays like *Shrimant, Manus Nawache Bet, AshiPakhare Yeti, Saree Ga Saree, Mi Jinkalo, Mi Haralo, Shantata: Court Chalu Ahe* and*MadhalyaBhint*'.

These plays move around the lives and concerns of lower-middle-class characters. These plays deal with financial crises, the issue of unemployment, and inadequate income of those with jobs, problems of housing and high rent, marriage and oppression of women and so on.

Having an exceptional ability, he develops a complete image of the characters with relative ease and sound details through few. His *Shrimant (*1955) exposes the traditional theme of the conflict between the rich and the poor in a capitalist society. There is also a depiction of the predicament of a lower-middle-class family with the problem of premarital pregnancy. *Shrimant*a and the subsequent *GharateAmucheChhan* unfold the rich who are morally lacking, corrupted, having a lust for money, and lead a selfish life. *Shantata! Court Chalu Ahe*, is one of the experimental and innovative play so far in Marathi theatre. In this play, Tendulkar has artistically introduced 'play within a play' and discloses real-life story. It is the combined world of fancy and fact by incorporating intense dramatic effects on it.

During the second period of a literary career, he shifted his focus from the middle-class setting to the socio-political and historical realm. To this period belong his noteworthy plays like *Gidhade* (1971*)*, *Sakharam Binder* (1972), *Ghashiram Kotwal* (1973), *Bhalyakaka* (1974), *Bhau Murarrao* (1975), and *Bebi* (1975). These plays appear to be full-fledged as compared to his early plays. *Ghashiram Kotwal*, one of the best creations and was greatly applauded and appreciated. It was performed in December 1972 and later published in 1973. This play is considered a bitter commentary on the hypocrisy of the dominant castes and classes in society. The play is set in the Peshwa period, and the characters are historical figures. But it is not a historical play. It depicts a fictional account of the social circumstances and characters like Ghashiram. The play is based on the revenge and Ghashiram's thirst for power that necessitate him to offer his daughter (Gauri) to Nana Phadanavis. This play also raised a bitter controversy and social protest in Pune. Nevertheless, the play was translated and staged in many languages in different regions and received not only national as well as global acclaim. Tendulkar has successfully employed chorus, kirtan, and folk music, and by giving such treatment to Marathi drama, he raised 'Marathiness'.

Ghashiram naturally establishes great aesthetic values as the play provides such multiple versions and a presentation.

Silence! The Court is in session and illuminated Tendulkar's career as a dramatist as well as the history of Marathi drama. The creation of New Woman in the play is new in terms of its matter and manner. Leela Benare, the protagonist, is a school teacher who has a free spirit and different attitude towards life, and hence the clash arises with strong defenders of patriarchy culture. Her soliloquy is one important issue that exposes her personal revelation in the play. The soliloquy is not a new device, but the playwright employs it by keeping a distance, and it raises many questions. The play depicts the pathetic position of women in the male-dominated Indian society. It also throws a flashlight on the fact of man-woman relationships and the place of an unmarried woman in male dominion. Shubha Tiwari's opinion is very appropriate and supportive to understand the play:

> The play poignantly portrays the plight, the ponderings, predicaments, and problems of a middle-class Indian woman. Society as a force is hostile to individual instincts as well as dignity. The very system of justice is gender biased. (35)

It is astounding to know that the play has been translated in fourteen Indian languagesand Tendulkar was honoured with the prestigious 'The Kamaladevi Chattopadhaya' award. The success of the play gifted him a placeon the national map as it was staged all over India in different versions. Tendulkar got recognition on the national level and this play widened the horizons of Marathi drama.

Tendulkar innovatively experimented with a dramatic structure in his play *AshiPakhare Yeti (So Come Birds).* This play is based on one Rain Maker of Romance. Vijay Tendulkar employed 'direct address' here. This dramatic device was new to the audience and to the Marathi stage during 1970-71. The protagonist, Arun Sarnaik addresses the audience directly and explains the course of the story.Later, this technique became regular usage in experimental Marathi theatre. The innovation not only confined to its presentation technique but also the love story between Arun and Saru echoes the poetic spiritual level at which their relationship develops. Tendulkar exercised the same innovative technique in the play *PahijeJatiche*(Wanted, Man of Right Caste) regarding its form and content. This thought-provoking play exposes corruption in the academic sector that spoils the life young boy. The story deals with a young man who belongs to the backward class. He studies well nurturing the ambition of becoming a college professor. But the young student fells to understand the dirty campus politics. As a result, he was terminated from the educational institute. The play reveals the burning issue of caste-based politics which has relevance even today.

Representing the burning subjects in his plays, his honest stand expressed in interviews, and the circumstances, Tendulkar always remained in controversy. He never cared for such criticism, and even sometimes his family was harassed. Many of his plays were expurgated, which probably was an obvious indication of the actual currency of incidents used in the plays and partly because of their strong rootedness in a socio-political context. On the contrary, the magnetic quality made these plays continue to be performed in different parts of India and abroad. It confirms that his plays have a strong appeal or certain universal quality, which might have attached and shocked audiences out of their complacency. Some people went to the extent of calling it a publicity stunt for living in a highlight of media. He clarifies his stand in an interview with Makarand Sathe, thus:

> I don't know about success; I don't know why people felt that way but I think I was very honest and responsible regarding my statements. And if you want to talk about success, I must have to submit that I am very successful to share my thoughts. (7)

The controversy remains a part of his career. It also raised its head with the projection of plays like *The Vultures, Sakharam Binder, Ghashiram Kotwal, Baby. The Vultures (Gidhade)* was actually written fourteen years before it was produced.It was published in a book-form and was staged in 1971. Actually speaking, Tendulkar's mind was preoccupied with the subject of *The Vultures* when he was writing *Shreemant* and*An Island Called Man.The Vultures* is an illustration of the structure of the family and familial relationship.Tendulkar employs the language or idiom so effectively into the play to expose the violence inside the family. He penetrates a general perception of the vulture in man, but its dramatic representation was refused. Tendulkar admitted that the characters of Ramakant and Umakant in the play are retained as he found them in real life. They were part of his personal life, so he was in a dilemma about the use of their names. Rama, the female character in the play, has to undergo anguish in life. She fell victim to the hands of men. Tendulkar himself felt surprised while watching *Vultures* on the stage. The play has been a powerful argument on violence, and the controversy was raised over the explicit language of the play.

When he brought *Silence! The Court is in Session*; the play equally shocked and astonished the audience. Here female internal life is exposed. The play moves around the central character, Leena Benare, who wants to create her own identity and existence. By employing devices like satire, irony, pathos, and mock elements in the play, Tendulkar exposes the duplicity and hypocrisy of a middle-class society that considers women as if she is an instrument for their pleasure.

Again, like *The Vulture*, Tendulkar focuses on human nature and investigates conflicts, sexual lust, and violence deep-rooted in men. His *Sakharam Binder* comes with its explosive subject matter and proves the first rash attempt play in the galaxy of Indian English drama. The main trait of the play is that Sakharam's outlook revolves around his lewdness, his women and their oppression, his use of power, and his ostensibly vulgar language. Each character of the play is a curious combination of strength and weakness, good and evil.

Here we find that Tendulkar does not take any specific moral stand, but he might not have done artistic detachment. The dramatic tension spontaneously takes its course among Sakharam, Laxmi, and Champa. The play aroused diverse reactions on the pretext of breaking the norms of orthodox society. The man-woman relationships portrayed here evoked bitter controversy. It is the story of a womanizer, Sakharam, and two women, Laxmi and Champa. These women having different tendencies, having a different attitude to life, enter his life.

Tendulkar's ambitious play, *Kamala,* is based on an actual newspaper report and shows a real-life incident about the auction of women at a village. The auction of women in a certain village represents the existence of the flesh trade of women. Ironically, the press conference is held where Kamala is asked vulgar questions. All this obviously reflects women's condition in a modern age. The title may hint at Kamala as the heroine of the play, but she is far from Shakespeare's heroine, like Rosalind in *As You Like It*. Kamala appears to be weak and poor, but it is she who opens the eyes of Sarita, wife of Jaisingh. Jaisingh, the press reporter, uses Kamala for his ambition. Through the sorry plight of Kamala, Tendulkar launches a bitter attack on the male-dominated Indian society, which gratifies on discriminating against the weaker sex.

The modern man's complex and manifold problems were very aptly presented by the playwright, and he did so by neglecting old values and norms. He is quite aware that the old values and outdated societal norms are not sufficient enough to expose the crisis of the modern man. Modern man is confused, disillusioned, and dehumanized, etc., for some reasons or others, and that modern man lacks optimism. That same perplexity of modern man finds its representative in the character of Arun in *Kanyadaan*. Like the other plays of Tendulkar, *Kanyadaan* is also a controversial play and called as anti-Dalit play. The play depicts social tensions caused by discrimination and casteism and how a girl (Seva) from a Brahmin family falls in love with a Dalit boy and how she lives in the house of Arun.

Themiddle-class life and middle-class ethos find their expression in Tendulkar's *An Obstinate Girl*. The conflict between the girl, Mangala and her father Tatya forms the subject matter. Mangala is a straightforward girl, Tatya is shy and hypocritical. But this supposedly superficial and conventional conflict has been provided new dimension by Tendulkar. Unfortunately, the play could not perform sufficient shows and hence failed to reach a wider audience. In the play *LobhNasava*(*Requested Not to Love*) one may witness a similar concept of interpersonal relationships, not only in the domestic circle but also among those who do not happen to be blood relations.

The extent of Vijay Tendulkar as a playwright lies in the fact that he entered a dramatic career without any thought out plan and yet became a successful dramatist in the world of literature. He has written various types of plays; just as plays for the radio, one-act plays, experimental plays, and even professional plays. He has also shown his multitalented skills in a variety of writings like stories for children, narrative fiction, scriptwriting, feature writing, translations, etc. However, his fame and popularity rest as a playwright. His plays might not have sustained concentration and intensity. His success lies in using the economy of words, expressing maximum meaning in minimum words; skilful handling of the subject and his innovative techniques are some of the striking features of his plays.

As a committed dramatist, Tendulkar never cared about blame or praise, success or failure. Therefore, he could experiment on content and form that appealed to him. His understanding of human life and compassion for women take place in his writings. He has mostly depicted the struggle of lost individuals against unfavorable circumstances or society. Having had great faith in his skill and passion, he never hesitated to express his humanistic approach and fearless attitude.

The problems of day-to-day life and some social issues find expression in his plays, but one cannot define his plays as 'problem plays' like plays of Ibsen, Shaw, or John Galsworthy. Tendulkar's plays expose several problems without providing any solution to them. He treats the drama as a tool of communication and interaction rather than a device for problems and solutions.The audience expects some solutions from Tendulkar, but he makes them troubled and ultimately compels them to ponder over the problems.

He portrays life as it is making little or no efforts to moralize or philosophize it. Therefore, the reader or audience does not receive any explicit message from his plays; rather, they are thought-provoking and elicit a silent protest in the minds of the audience. Like the playwrights, Arthur Miller, Shaw, Eugene O'Neill, etc., Tendulkar also greatly succeeded in entertaining the audience and instructing them with devices like irony, mockery, and contradictions. His plays necessitate the audience to keep himself in the context. Even though the plays depict misery, suffering, and the helplessness of man, the plays are called anti-sentimental and anti-emotional. Like Aristotle's terminology of drama, Vijay Tendulkar succeeds in evoking the emotion of pity and terror since pathos and violence characterize most of the action in the plays. Asha Kanwar rightly remarks that:

> The effect produced by the play can be seen as neither one of 'empathy' as in the dramatic form of theatre nor one of 'alienation' as in the epic form of theatre but also akin to the Theatre of Cruelty so that the audience can understand the social process that leads to violence and cruelty, a malaise that Tendulkar has studied as a research project and effectively depicted in artistic form in his plays. (52)

The issues of women and despairs of powerless and feeble human beings appear to be the basic themes of Tendulkar's plays. At the end of the nineteenth century, we find some problems like the early marriage of girls, polygamy, a sale of girls for marriage, strict restrictions on widows, education, confinement to domestic and child-rearing, etc. Consequences: women suffered a lot. Tendulkar attempts to highlight the same picture of harsh reality in his plays. If we study the plays, we will see two contrary types of women characters in the play; in the first type, we have sensitive, generous, and tender-hearted Indian women, and in the second category, women are assertive, rebellious, and dominant. The characters like Laxmi, Kamala, and Rama belong to the first category of women who calmly accept the condition. On the other hand, the characters like Leela Benare, Sarita, Champa, and Jyoti are fully conscious of injustice and exploitation. So they represent rebellious nature. He exposes women's characters with compassion and a humanistic approach in the plays that show his sympathy towards the weak and pathetic situation of women. It proves that Tendulkar is a strong supporter of freedom, equality, and social justice for all. Like Anton Chekhov, he would have refined, integrated, and awakened the world.

With the help of imaginative realism, Tendulkar portrayed burning and particularly sensitive issues of women and contemporary. He strove to penetrate into characters and tried to find how life functions at different layers. The degradation of moral values due to power in the modern political system reveals various dimensions in his plays. The game of power is unfurled in plays like *Silence! The Court is in session, Kamala, Sakharam Binder*, *Kannaydan,* and *Ghashiram Kotwal.* Most of the plays concentrate on the status of women in a patriarchal society, and the evils like power politics, the battle for supremacy, and brutal relationships are treated through gender relations.

Marathi drama during Tendulkar's lifetime was worn out by propaganda for political awakening and cheap and vulgar entertainment. Tendulkar becomes a pioneer in the sense that he has guided the Marathi drama that had lost its proper track. Having molded the external structure of Marathi plays, Tendulkar has gifted immortality to his characters. He was realistic enough to portray an imaginative world or superficial conflicts. He delved deep into the real-world effects. Like William Shakespeare, the place of Vijay Tendulkar as a playwright will remain everlasting in the annals of Marathi literature and Indian drama. In this context, Ulhas Luktuke's comment is quite significant:

> Tendulkar‘s plays broaden the ambit of the Marathi plays. He gives expression to the banality of everyday life of common people in a dramatic form. After the successful presentation of *Silence! The Court is in Session*, he brings psychological realism in his plays through the discussion of various problems. He has fathered a new world of sensibility. That is his greatest contribution to Marathi Literature and Theatre. (9)

Writer and playwright Vijay Tendulkar, whose vallentdelineation of socially controversial themes changed traditional Marathi theatre. This world class figure passed away on 19 May, 2009 in Pune. He was 80 and was suffering from myasthenia gravis — a muscular disorder. Tendulkar was in hospital for the past month and a half — was in a "critical" condition. The playwright, who was born in 1928, was survived by daughters Sushma and Tanuja. He was cremated in Pune without rituals or funeral speeches, as was his wish.

Vijay Tendulkar is an extraordinary, skilled dramatist. He has modified the shape of Indian drama with his mighty pen and his intellectual power. With the translation of the works in English and other languages, Tendulkar has been recognized as an effective force in contemporary English drama. His plays created quite a swirl in the literary circle. Themes, structures, and dialogues of his plays hold the attention of the scholars and researchers. As a result, many scholars' present research papers and articles in numerous journals, magazines, and newspapers, and few of the research scholars have submitted their doctoral theses on his dramatic work. Therefore, the researcher takes a decision to have a glance at a brief review of some of the research articles, papers, works, etc. on his plays.

The drama is one of the forms of literature that require an audience. It does not exist in isolation or vacuum. Drama is a product of the social and political milieu that surrounds it; in turn, it exerts an influence on the milieu. To understand the drama, it requires some knowledge of conditions outside the playhouse. So, Tendulkar focuses on the relationships within and outside the family and brings out their connectivity and complications. Isolation comes from defiance of accepted institutions, individuals, and society. Modern literature is full of isolation, and relationships are within a decaying moral order. He protests against it.

Tendulkar never involves himself to highlight false idealism or feelings of nationalism or patriotism. His characters are typical individuals, and they strike a blow, to the fullest, to establish social norms or religious convictions. They require space for themselves in the society, which the society is unwilling to share with them. One of the features of Tendulkar's plays is thought-provoking. They ignite the minds of the audience and protest against the evils and vices of society. To raise his voice against the carnage and against the oppression of innocents, Tendulkar intelligently employs the drama as a medium.

Tendulkar grasps the complex issues skilfully. He protests against adultery, hypocrisy, dual personality, vulgarity, cruelty, narrow-mindedness, violence, distorted relations, breakdown of a joint family system, faithlessness, and oppression of women in modern society. Major issues of life like psychological, socio-political, existential, feminist, and humanitarian are delineated in a realistic manner. His presentation of stark realities staggered the orthodox Indian society, which was unable to assimilate it. As a result, they protested against Tendulkar, and many times the playwright faced controversy.

An inspection of contemporary Indian drama reveals the works of Trinity. Vijay Tendulkar, Girish Karnad, and Mahesh Dattani represent influential and resurgent Indian theater. One of the things that profoundly amalgamate them is their mutually complementary treatment of the problematic of contemporary Indian subjectivity on the various axes of gender, sexuality, history, politics, tradition, class, and socio-cultural change. With their innovative visions and experiments, these playwrights have given new directions to modern Indian drama.

Vijay Tendulkar as a Feminist

Literature is also one of the media that shows various aspects of life. It also reflects the feminist concept and values effectively. Feminist elements reflect in all the plays composed by a great dramatist, Vijay Tendulkar. The plays are contained with feminist elements to a great deal.

Although Tendulkar denied himself as a feminist, his leanings and sympathies towards female characters in his plays proved him a great feminist. Even he gives the role of protagonist to female characters. This makes the researcher choose the subject. The word feminist comes from feminism, which originally meant simply being feminine, and the latter got the meaning advocacy of women's rights in 1980. A feminist is someone who advocates for or supports equal rights for women. If your brother objects strongly to women being paid less than men for doing the same job, he is a feminist. If you believe that women should have the same political, social, and economic rights as men, you are a feminist. This helps us to prove Tendulkar as a feminist because his representations of women characters evidence that he indirectly supports them to raise a voice against subjugation. He is as conscious of his role as a playwright and as a sensitive human being. He admits:

> The writer in me is more analytical than emotionally committed one way or the other. The writer in me raises inconvenient question instead of choosing his side and passionately claiming thereafter that it is always the right one...As a social being I am against all exploitation and passionately fell that all exploitation must end. (Agrawal 25)

As the study attempts to study Vijay Tendulkar's women characters in the light of feminism, his portrayal of women requires to be studied from a feminist perspective. As an author of the post-independent period, he reflects a realistic picture of the contemporary educated, middle-class, urban Indian woman. His plays portray the despondent plight of the contemporary middle-class, urban Indian woman and also analyze how the patriarchy has not changed much even in the twentieth century. Despite his vehement denial of being a feminist, Tendulkar has made bold attempts at giving a voice to the suffering and frustrations of women.

Tendulkar denies calling himself a feminist. There may be many reasons, but one of the basic reasons is that he does not restrict himself to one ideology, which is feminism, or maybe he is a man, and he is not in the mind to face one controversy of a male-dominated world. In the twenty-first century, there is a strong debate about whether feminism is required to study or there is no need for it.

Furthermore, to understand Vijay Tendulkar's position as a feminist, one must have a perusal of reader response theory. Reader response theory proposes certain approaches to literature. First, it advocates the aesthetic response to the work of art or literature. Secondly, the theory postulates that a literary text should be decoded and interpreted according to the intention, ideology, socio-economic milieu, and other influences of the author. Thirdly, and importantly, literary text should be interpreted and decoded from the perspective of the reader. The theory, as its name indicates, gives primacy to the reader, who plays a vital role in interpreting and bringing out the meaning from a text.

As per the theory, meaning neither exists in the text nor in the author's mind; rather, exists within the reader. Readers use various outlooks and perceptions while reading a text. The reader employs his own experience. Reading becomes a process that comes across three meaningful facets that set the basis of the relationship between reader and text. It is the process of anticipation and retrospection, the consequent revealing of the text as a living phenomenon, and the consequent impression of lifelikeness. Reading is, thus, a creative process. The different readers use their different skills and varied impressions of the text. Mere dexterous narrative techniques of the author cannot reveal the complete picture before the reader. It is only the reader who can absorb and interpret the world of the text.

> The process of reading enables the reader to unravel what is the unsaid and unwritten part of the text and executes the balancing act by maintaining the levels of interpretation. Thus, a reader plays a vital role in the process of constructing, assigning, and interpreting meaning. It is the interaction between the text and the reader that generates meaning. The study of Tendulkar's plays in the light of reader response theory enables us to announce Tendulkar as a great feminist.

As we know that the women characters are portrayed with great understanding and compassion, though Tendulkar is not a self-acknowledged feminist. Shanta Ghokale rightly points out:

> They are not romanticized, idealized, or forced to live by their creator's symbolic purposes. They are a first and foremost human being of flesh and blood who draws their features from the widest range of observed examples. They are allowed to inhabit the entire spectrum from the malleable to the stubborn, from the conservative to the rebellious from the self –sacrificing to the grasping. (81)

Tendulkar has artistically portrayed the plight and predicament of women in the urban middle-class society. He has variously dealt with the varied dimensions of man's cultural deformity and brought out its effect on a man-woman relationship. Culture and biology distinguish human beings that further divide human beings into two classes: men and women. Tendulakar's plays understudy *Silence: the Court is in Session, Sakhram Binder,* and *Kamala*depict Tendulkar's ideology of feminism. These plays demonstrate how women are humiliated, exploited, and marginalized in the male-dominated society. The dramatist not merely exposes gender inequality but seeks a solution to it. He treats his female protagonists with great comprehension and sympathy. The female characters in his plays reveal his intensive treatment of themes like social conscience and complex human relationships. He has presented his characters in a natural form. He exposes the deprivation, humiliation, commodification, and suppression of women due to patriarchal society through his female characters, thereby exploring the plight and misery of women in the past as well as in contemporary Indian society. Tendulkar gives female characters protagonist roles in his plays. They belong to different statuses and backgrounds, but they are fixed for the same treatment by the male-dominated society. It shows his inclinations towards feminism.

Tendulkar's dramatic world is women-centric, where he unfurls the pains, sufferings, and fragmented selves of women on account of gender discrimination and exploitation. *Silence! The Court is in Session and* unfolds the sorry reality of ill-treatment given to women. It lashes a blow to the male-dominated society where a woman serves merely as an object of wish fulfillment. His *Kamala* depicts the life of a woman, Kamala, who is sold in a rural flesh market. This gyno-centric play discusses the trivial existence of a woman in male-dominated Indian society. The play is based on a newspaper story, and Tendulkar has made skillful use of it to expose the social evil of patriarchy. These plays show Tendulkar's strong belief in feminism. *Sakharam Binder* exposes the representative male ego, which treats women as mere commodities under the pretext of benevolence. Like the other feminists, he too believes that the same rights, power, and opportunities should be granted to women. In his plays, it is around women that most of the action revolves.

The three plays analyzed herein focus on the female protagonists who are consistently exploited by a misogynistic society and are bearing their travails with resilience and stoicism. These heroines successfully challenge the patriarchal conventions prevalent in society that compel them to destroy their identity and their self-respect. The ways of challenges taken up by each of these women are different; however, what binds them is their common enemy, viz., 'patriarchy', and their common end, viz., 'independence'.

His *Silence! The Court is in Session, Sakharam Binder* and *Kamala* are true documents that serve to unravel women's exploitation on the one hand and female awakening on the other. The portrayal of women characters appears to be that of feminists who are passive, weak, and oppressed by male- dominance at the beginning, but in the course of time, they become self-empowered, ready to defy the oppressive system of patriarchy. These plays are very significant as far as a feminist point of view. Tendulkar portrays humiliation, abuse, oppression, and the indignity of women in the 21st century, where women are still treated as subordinates on account of their gender.

Vijay Tendulkar is not a rebellious feminist. He believes that we are all part of society, and we cannot live alone; we have to live in it; we need a family and some ties. More than being a feminist, he is a humanist. His views are more akin to modern feminist thought, which is no longer regarded as radical. He expresses his desire to be a humanist

After independence, it is certainly true that the Indian women gained considerable importance within their country in social and political spheres. They took many progressive decisions, such as organizing themselves to fight for a new set of goals. They also acquired political position, and as an effect, they could take decisions. The goals were getting equality based on gender, job opportunities, reforming the existing law, which gave women only partial justice, and creating a society that did not suppress women intellectually, physically, and emotionally. However, some new issues have taken birth with changing the course.

The significance of feminism in the Indian context cannot be overstated, as almost half of the population is being isolated from the mainstream and holds a subordinate position in society. Although much water has flown under the pool during the past, still traces of some problems remain, and new issues crop up in a modern age. Even after some 70 years of independence, the condition of women is far from satisfactory in India. Some of the critics today undermine the requirement of feminism, but problems of women are increasing day after day in India.

Although sex-ratio is increased, the incidents of child abuse, child-marriages, marriages of young girls by their parents against their will, hundreds of brides are being killed or burnt alive by their in-laws, and dowry system is rampant in society. Moreover, stigmas like rape, gang rape, and sexual harassment occur in day to day life as common events all over the country. In order to tackle such problems, the study of feminism along with its manifold aspects is desirable.

The struggle to establish equality for women with men has almost become a paradigm in the nation. On the contrary, the members of patriarchy are exploiting every measure to ensure a continuation of their age-old superiority and dominance over women. The Bill for a one-third reservation of seats in Parliament and Assemblies in India for women is still waiting to be passed. This is sheer proof of total reluctance to let women progress towards equality. The 'second sex' still have to face and compete with outdated anti-women laws, customs, and traditions such as divorce, dowry, inheritance, abortion, rape, etc.They fall victims of such harsh reality. It is evident that women have silently suffered and endured humiliation for centuries. Their reliance on men and the submission to ill-fate have touched the very core of psychology of the majority of women, illiterate as well as literate. Therefore, there is a great necessity of reforms expected from all reformers in order to materialize women's emancipation in a real sense. Although social progress and enlightened women's efforts have succeeded in bringing about some desirable changes, still many more things remain to be achieved.

Today we are living in the age of globalization and we talk about India as a developing country yet, ironically, some basic subjects like the environment, gender equality, women's emancipation, and women's empowerment remain burning issues in India. This fact necessitates man to think and have a solution to such problems. As for the women, empowerment is concerned; some rudimentary questions cloud our mind. The questions are like, after seventy years of independence, the women are not really emancipated, they are not independent in reality, they do get equal treatment, our society still discriminates on the basis of gender, education does not improve or upgrade their condition, they are not safe or secure, etc.

Literature holds as a mirror of human life. Although it is supposed to be a vague concept having abstract significance or totally divorced from the life that dwells in the land of fancy and imagination, it is the reflection of reality. It is a reflection that has a direct link with life and its realities. Creative literature grows out of the real situations and events of life, and without creative and constructive literature, life has no inner significance. Literature is one of the routes. Once the daily requirements are fulfilled, man allows his curiosity to explore the mysteries of life. The curiosity for knowledge and the desire to understand life make one feel at home in the universe. Literature has many genres. But the drama has been very influential and powerful because of its audio-visual medium of expression. It constitutes a very important part of the literature. "Whenever and wherever the humans have progressed beyond the mere struggle for existence, God's recreation, and self-expression, there has been a theater in some sense" (Tiwari.1).

A number of scholars and critics find explanations of women's status, their humiliation, as well as victimization by the male-dominated society in Tendulkar's three plays, *Silence! The Court is in Session*, *Sakharam Binder*, and *Kamala.* A number of critics scrutinized Tendulkar's plays and explored various aspects of his plays. The main focus of critics appears on such thematic concerns as violence, exploitation of women, deterioration of man-woman relations, social problems, power, politics, and the patriarchy system. There are also many essays and research articles that study Tendulkar's plays in the light of psychological and social aspects. Some researchers feel that Tendulakar's plays have illustrated the place and wretched condition of women. Though the critics have studied Tendulkar's plays in the perception of feminism, they have not achieved a deep level of this aspect so far. Therefore, it is essential to analyze and study Tendulkar's play in order to assess his projection of women and their situation in his plays. It is also important to study his sympathies and his inclinations towards women as reflected in all different forms in his plays. All the limitations, disparities, and gaps regarding existing studies of Tendulkar as a feminist require a comprehensive assessment of its different dimensions.

The present book is a humble attempt to explore and establish the feasibility of probing this neglected aspect, viz., Tendulkar, as a feminist. This book will precisely explain Tendulkar's stance as a feminist. The word 'feminist' can be interpreted in varied ways. In its general sense, it indicates the person who backs feminism and fights for equality in every walk of life. A feminist may be one who condemns, defies, opposes, or revolts against the variety of distinctions and discriminations against women. The discriminations against women in terms of gender now and then evoke a good deal of discussions and debates among sociologists, philosophers, psychologists, and scholars.

As per feminists, in order to understand a woman's situation in this world, it is essential that one should be acquainted with the term patriarchy. The patriarchal system is one that assumes and bestows man as rational, bold, aggressive, dominating, independent, fearless, and having the ability to rule and control others. On the other hand, women are deemed to be timid, passive, self-sacrificing, docile, submissive, emotional, and dutiful towards their husbands and family members. This system relies upon the notion of hierarchical binaries of genders, man's superiority, and woman's inferiority. It grants to man to assert domination in every possible form, apparently, in order to sustain balance in marriage and family.

The negative qualities are assigned to the woman and her counterpart. A man is always in an advantageous position; he is in the right, while a woman is in the wrong. It indicates that a man is afraid of feminine competition. While discussing sexual initiation, sexual pleasure, etc., De Beauvoir states that a woman is not a free agent in choosing the man of her erotic lot. She says that a man is ever inconsistent and wants his wife to be passionate with him but indifferent to others. He wants her absolutely his. In this way, the woman is betrayed from the very day of marriage. She remains bound to one man, with children to tend; a woman's life is over. She considers her being in terms of her husband. De Beauvoir further remarks that the relation between man and woman should be based on common love and consent and women should be freed from the bonds of slavery. Jawaharlal Nehru opined that "you can tell the condition of a nation by looking at the status of its women" (Sharma 1). Undoubtedly, a woman of any nation is the mirror of its civilization. Where she enjoys equal status, we may say that society has reached a level of maturity and sense of responsibility.

It is also an important time; therefore, every citizen should think for a while about women's condition, not just as denial but for serious reflection and to be one with forces of women's equality. The fact must be accepted that we are living in a patriarchaleloped elaborated systems governing all spheres of life over centuries, society whose intrinsic structure is based on gender discrimination. We have developed elaborated systems governing all spheres of life over centuries. Despite the social reform movements and statutory provisions, patriarchy rules in our society. Discrimination begins even before the very birth.

Works Cited

Agrawal, Beena.*Dramatic World of VijayTendulkar Exploration and Experimentations*. Jaipur: Aadi publications, 2012. Print.

Banerjee, Arundhati. "Introduction",*Fiveplays of Vijay Tendulkar*. Bombay: OUP, 1992.Print.

Barat, Urvashi,*When Writing is Life Itself*. New Delhi: Asia Book Club, 2002 Print.

Chitnis, Suma. *Alphabet of Lust*. Kenyan Review, Vol. VIII. 1951. Print.

De Beauvoir, Simone. *The Second Sex*. Harmondsworth: Penguin, 1952. Print.

Gokhale, Shanta. "Tendulkar on His Own Terms", Vijay Tendulkar in conversation with Shanta Gokhale, *KATHA* publication, New Delhi: 2001. Print.

---."Born with the theatre" The Hindu, October 15, 2000.Print.

Jardine, Alice. *Gynesis: Configurations of Women and Modernity*. Ithaca: Cornell U.P, 1986.Print.

Kanwar, Asha S. *Ghashiram Kotwal: A Study Guide*. New Delhi: IGNOU, 1993.Print.

Lai, Malashri. *Women Writers in Indian English*. Simla: Indian Institute of Advanced Study, 1995. Print.

Luktuke, Ulhas."Abhar! RangachyaEwadhyaTukadyasathi",*Kesari*, Translated by Shailaja Wadekar Mar.29, 1970. Print.

Nayantara, Uma. *Indian Women writer's at the Cross Roads*. New Delhi: Pen crafts, 1996. Print.

Nehru, Jawaharlal. *The Discovery of India.*Centenary edition. Delhi: Oxford U.P, 1989. Print.

Offen, Karen. "Defining Feminism: a comparative historical approach" *Beyond Equality and Difference: Citizenship, Feminist Politics, and Female Subjectivity.* Eds. Gisela Bock and Susan James. London: Routledge, 1999. Print.

Sathe, Dr.Makarand. "Tendulkar and violence-Then and Now,"Interview with VijayTendulkar. Print.

Smith, Nicholas D. "Plato and Aristotle on the Nature of Women".*Journal of the History of Philosophy.* **21** *(4)(1983): 467–478.*

Ramnarayan, Gauri, "View From The Balcony", Vijay Tendulkar in conversation with Gowri Ramnarayan", *KATHA* publication, New Delhi, 2001. Print.

Sharma, Swati. *Status of Women in India.* New Delhi: Pearl Books, 2007. Print.

Tiwari, Subha."Silence! The Court is in Session: A Strong Social Commentary" *Contemporary of Indian Dramatists.* Ed. Shubha Tiwari. New Delhi: Atlantic Publisher, 2007.Print.

West, Rebecca. *The Young Rebecca: Writing of Rebecca West* -1911-1917. ed. Jane Marcus London: Macmillan, 1982. Print.

4 *Silence! The Court is in Session:* Patriarchal Society and Exploitation

Patriarchy, as it is called, is assumed to be the principal obstacle to women's progress and advancement. Therefore, it is essential to understand the system that relegates women to subordinate status and to unravel its workings in order to work for women's development in a systematic way. In the modern world where women reach in the space by their potentials and their merit, but patriarchy appears that created barriers for women in their progress in society.

The present chapter deals with the concept of patriarchal society, its implication in the Indian context, and the exploitation of women. Patriarchal society is reflected in Tendulkar's famous and applauded play *Silence! The Court is in Session* (STCIS). This chapter is an attempt to analyze the concept of patriarchy and how a woman gets a subordinate position from a theoretical perspective. As a playwright and antagonist of patriarchy, Tendulkar puts forth his views in this play. The researcher studies this chapter in the light of Vijay Tendulkar as a feminist.

The concept 'patriarchy' exactly means the rule of the father or the 'patriarch', and originally it was used to describe a specific type of'male-controlled family'. The large household of the patriarch family included women, junior men, children, slaves, and domestic servants; all were under the rule of this dominant male. So, we can define patriarchy as a structure of social relations between men and women, which have a material base and which, though hierarchical, establish or create independence and cohesion among men that permit them to dominate women.

The patriarchal culture, customs, institutions, and social relations are structured in such a way that women obtain the inferior or secondary position in the society. Granting complete priority to men, women's human rights are boundrs to the male authority both in public and private spheres and suppressed. It refers to the male authority both in public and private spheres. Thus, feminists strongly oppose patriarchal society. Feminism employs the term 'patriarchy' to explore the relationship between men and women. They have discovered that patriarchal society is the root cause of women's radicalization, subjugation, and oppression. Particularly, Raal feminists strongly oppose such culture and consider it a thinstitution of all evils against women. It insists that society, the titutuion family, the hierarchical restructuring of society, and sex roles themselves must be restructured for the demolition of patriarchy.

Second-wave feminism came in the early1960s and lasted roughly two decades and quicly spread across the Western world. The feminist writings of the 1970's and 1980's raised questions about female condition and sought to find out the influence of patriarchy, not just in politics and the economy but in all aspects of social, personal and sexual existence which certifies male superiority and female inferiority.Kate Millet asserted this idea in her book*Sexual Politics*(1970)in which she defined the "patriarchal government"as an institution "whereby that half of the population which is female is controlled by the half which is male" (Heywood 240).

In reality, Male members hold power and prevail in a family, and in the society. They also take an interest in political leadership and moral authority. Men seize social privilege and property in Patriarchy social system. In patriarchal society property and title are inherited by the male lineage. Primarily adult men hold the authority or power and women merely follow the order of men. This clarification of patriarchal society elucidates that patriarchy is a society, culture or community where men rule and privilege, and women are considered as subordinate.

Speaking mostly, patriarchy detains 'rule of the father' and is constructed socially and ideologically. It believes men as superior and powerful to women in many respects. By considering men as superior to women, men hold power in their hands. This system is full of injustice, inhuman and unequal. So, it helps men directly or indirectly to restrain women's production, reproduction, and sexuality. As a result, human divides into two class; masculine and feminine character stereotypes in the society. Power relations are the core of the system and it strengthens the iniquitous power relations between men and women. However, patriarchy is not constant. It has changed over the periods of history. In the process of change, gender relations have undergone dynamic and complex phase.

Women are kept in a subordinate position in a number of ways in this social system. We can experience subordination of women at a daily level, regardless of the class we might belong to, takes various forms – discrimination, exploitation, disregard, bitter comments from men, insult, control, oppression, violence – within the family, at the place of work, at the public places, in society.

A few examples must be observed here that represent a specific form of discrimination and a particular aspect of patriarchy. Such as, son preference, finds discrimination against girls in job opportunities, food distribution, burden of household work on women and young girls, lack of freedom and mobility for girls, lack of educational opportunities for girls, lack of inheritance or property rights for women, wife battering, male control over women and girls, male control over women's bodies and sexuality, no control over fertility or reproductive rights.

The male dominance and discrimination towards women not only make women's lives miserable but also disturb their mental peace in a patriarchal society. It has a typical character of the feudal structure having a legacy of the medieval period. The social base of patriarchy lies in a socio-religious system. In the feudal system, the aristocratic class holds the top of a ladder and the sufferer at the bottom. Those who are on the top of the ladder exploit the women and downtrodden classes sexually and economically. Consequently, many times violence takes place. Since harassment and exploitation of women are part of this system.

It is very important to increase the dependency of women. So the existing social and political order has envisaged many ways. The patriarchal family and society are the single most powerful unit that denies her access to law and keeps her propertyless. It instructs women with a multiplicity of conceptions and misconceptions concerning their gender and role in society and family. This process of indoctrination has gained so much power to men that women tend to relate it as natural:

> Through the slow magic of time, such customs by long repetition become second nature in the individual. If he violates them, he faces certain fear, discomfort or shame; this is the origin of conscience or moral sense which Darwin chose as the most impressive distinction between animals and man. (Durrant 36)

We are familiar with Indian customs and traditions, and it is part and parcel of the Indian social structure in which patriarchy still goes on. The hegemony of patriarchy intensely stays alive in traditional Indian society. The woman is a mirror of society, and societal expressions are to be accepted as she is an inevitable part of family structure. The patriarchal society has created such a structured mechanism that women are treated badly all over the world.

We can also see the same structure in the Indian context. In Indian society, a woman has long been regarded either as a Pativrata Nari (means a pious and pure lady who worships her husband and follows his order) or a Veshya (prostitute). The society does not permit the emergence of a third independent category of women. Whenever a woman tries to break traditional confinement, which may help her to create a new identity for herself other than the conventionally available positions of ineffectual or a mistress, society collectively makes efforts and draws the boundary line in order to restrain her. The same boundary line made by patriarchal society is found in the play. People of the society are habituated only to tolerate the dumb dolls around.

Social institutes work against women and compel them to be in the second position. Institutes such as school, court, education, language, family, and marriage provide a motivational and conducive atmosphere for men to make use of women. The society acts in such a way that women unknowingly accept and become part of it. It empowers men and simultaneously makes women weak. There is a long history of women's suffering in the male-oriented society.

In this patriarchal society, men and women are institutionalized differently. So, they act, behave, think, and aspire in a different way. They have been instructed to think of masculinity and femininity in ways in which conditions find the difference. It considers or accepts that men have, or should have, one set of qualities, capacities, and characteristics and women have another. It is believed that man has strength, bravery, fearlessness, dominance, and competitiveness qualities, while the woman has caring, nurturing, love, timidity, and obedience qualities. It is clear that women are victims of subordination (e.g., under male dominance), exploitation (e.g., unequal pay, low wages), and oppression (e.g., violence) in our country. To understand the role of women in society, it is essential to quote the comment of Elise Boulding:

> The image of women in the earliest human history is that of a . . . food-gathering, child-bearing-breast-feeding female . . . who is both protected and victimized by the brute strength of the male, who gains the brief respite as mother-goddess and monarch—then loses all claims to power and status as a man invents the plough and takes over farming. (Thankamma 80-81)

The logic of male theory is linked with the logic of patriarchy. The male mind is conditioned as superior to the female body; therefore, we see that in actual life, women are engaged in household work and men are assigned intellectual work. The condition of women in the marriage market highlights secondary status. Alfred Lord Tennyson, the Victorian poet, in his poem *The Princess* voices the reality when he composes that man made for the field and the woman, for the hearth. The Victorian prejudice believes that it is a man who has the power to handle the sword and women should do such work as sewing by the needle. The Victorian prudery further attributes man with the quality of intellect and woman with the heart. They think that man is made to command and woman to obey. On these premisesink that man is made tarecommannd woman to obey man-woman relations is based on.

Tradition and custom are the souls of Indian society, and the caste factor plays a crucial role in every sphere of human life. People cannot break easily the limitations of Indian society. They follow blindly without any scientific base. The patriarchy has prevailed in our society right from the ancient Vedic period. Take two instances of the Ramayana and *Mahabharata that* contain the patriarchal culture through different angles.

The epics contain the role of a woman who presented ideal conduct and models for womanhood. But these models also have ingrained themselves in the subordination of the women. Some women figures are important in both epics.

Sita is a paragon of beauty and virtue. Being an ideal wife, she serves her husband with complete devotion. Draupadi presents to us an ideal of womanhood. She is learned, iron and revengeful, intolerant towards humiliation. She is a counselor, perfect wife, and companion of her husband. Among the other learned women of the epic, we may find Kunti, Sumitra, Gandhari, and Kaikeyi. These women left their influence on Indian society. So, men see women through such a culture.

Tendulkar is one of the playwrights who finds his characters first and then cultivates his own ideas. He cannot begin writing his plays with his idea or theme in mind. He also admits, "I had to have my characters first with me... as living persons leading me into the thick of their lives where they would give me the theme" (Gokhale 80). It suggests that Tendulkar depicts in his plays whatever he has found in living male or female. He never exposes his characters with imaginative eyes. His characters are first and foremost human beings of flesh and blood who get into the real world.

Vijay Tendulkar has artistically dealt with the Indian social system. He has depicted the patriarchal system in his plays: *Kamala, Sakharam Binder, and Silence! The Court is in Session, Kanydaan,* and *The Vulture.* These plays show how women are exploited and subjugated by this society. His projection of patriarchy is based on social reality and on straightforward social inspection.

Tendulkar uses a satire artistically on contemporary society to reveal the hollowness of patriarchal society and the status of women in the play. He focuses on gender deformity that suppresses women at all the levels of gender, class, caste, etc. Similarly, he has attacked all the social institutions and establishments, such as, family, marriage, the workplace, and so on. The play itself evidences feminist ideology. Feminists revolt against the patriarchy that prevails in human society. This element of feminist has been truly exposed in the play.*Silence! The Court is in*

Session. In this play, Tendulkar has made it clear that exploitation and subordination of women are caused by patriarchal society, and he tries to eradicate them through the character of Leela Benare.

The problem of unmarried mothers is a result of the mindset of people, modernization, and rapid socioeconomic change. The resultant collapse of the moral order systems leads to the disintegration of traditional social values. Indian people even now practice segregation of the sexes. They strongly believe in the purity and chastity of women. Still, they deny unmarried girls and treat such women badly and in an inhumane way. Actually, a woman is not only responsible for raising the problem, but she also has to face difficulties and suffering.

This is another problem related to girls, and it requires much greater attention than it has received so far from both legal agencies and voluntary welfare organizations. It is essential to provide adequate assistance to such women for their children and their rehabilitation. There must be counseling centers that persuade families and people to take a more humane view of this problem. So, unmarried girls can save from committing suicide or becoming prostitutes. Vijay Tendulkar, as a sensitive playwright, focuses on the same issue in this play.

Miss Banare is one of the dominant female characters in the play. Being modern and possessing a free spirit, she thinks outside of the patriarchal society. But patriarchal society neither lets her grow up enough nor allows her to live life happily. She is courageous to confront successfully against the male-dominated society, but at last, she loses her battle. The society has too deep the mechanism of gender bias that even the apparently liberal representatives of her society confirm to be the efficient critics of female emancipation. The play reveals dark aspects of patriarchy culture and the crafty game of the people in an artistic manner. The play moves around Benare's personal life.

Silence! The Court is in Session: The Play at a Glance

Silence! The Court is in Session, has been the translation of Tendulkar's play *Shantata! Court Chaule Ahe*(1967). The play was translated from the Marathi language by Priya Adarkar. The play is the strong exposure of patriarchal society that gives birth to an apathetic condition for the woman. Tendulkar has depicted the exploitation of a young woman in patriarchal culture, who becomes a victim of the male-dominated society. Tendulkar has criticized the follies prevailing in society.

The play represents a modern society that gangs up on a woman who has a child out of wedlock and how people suppress, oppress, subjugate, and compel her to commit suicide. Her attempts to raise a voice against patriarchal society become futile due to male dominance. Without mercy, sympathy, or pity for a woman, people in the theater group only enjoy teasing and exploiting her. It reveals their attitude towards a woman as well as their sadist tendency.

Discussing the problem of unmarried woman motherhood and showing the conflict between individual and society, the playwright introduces the feminist element (patriarchal culture), which is much in high pitch. He has depicted the exploitation of a woman and her struggle in patriarchal society in an inventive manner. Tendulkar's creative force is realistic and equally convincing. According to N. Sharda Iyer, "It has been seen as the first significant modern Indian play in any language to center on a woman as protagonist and victim, locates its heroine, Leela Benare, not at an acquiescent receiving end, but at a point of conflict, whereas as an as an aggressive transgressor of the sexual mores of her community, she challenges the executors or power in absentia" (159). In order to examine patriarchal culture and exploitation in this play, a careful analysis has been made in this chapter.

After independent India, the play was set in modern India. The Indian Constitution provides equal rights to everyone, irrespective of caste, creed, race, sex, or gender. Tendulkar is aware of a real-life situation. Being a human and feminist, he exposes the problem in the play. In this world, women are still extremely vulnerable and subject to the most dangerous, both in the private and public spheres.

The plays of Vijay Tendulkar feel like a mirror that reflects the serious and harsh realities of life and arouses an awareness of the perpetual realities of contemporary Indian life. As we know in the patriarchy, a victim is known, always a woman, because love is only a passing episode in a man's life, but to a woman, it is her very existence and her life. She sacrifices herself while loving someone else. The same happens in the life of Benare. She loves both men from the bottom of her heart, but they love Benare for physical pleasure. Here the playwright reveals the condition in patriarchal society. Jasbir Jain's statement effectively sums up the present state of feminist struggle in India:

> ...while feminism has generated awareness, created space, intervened in legislation, values, and structures continue to be patriarchal and the tradition continues to define roles and respectability, especially in traditional societies like ours. (91)

It is true that women have been treated as a commodity in society since long. Sometimes women are used as a commercial device, sometimes for stepping stone and sometimes for sexual pleasure. Tendulkar reflects the same condition of women characters in his plays. Exemplar is Nana Phadanvis, in Tendulkar's' *Ghashiram Kotwal* who enjoys Gulabi'sLavani(folk art) Show. At the same time, he wants to have sex with a teenage girl, Gauri. Phadanvis'sbehavioural patternaccentuates that women are only for the entertainment of men. Tendulkar's other play*Sakharam Binder* backs the concept that a man needs a woman for sexual pleasure. Sakharam does not believe in other responsibility rather he would satisfy the hunger of his body. Similarly, Kamala is used as a professional tool for Jaisingh in *Kamala*. In *Silence! The Court is in Session*Miss Leela Benare is seduced by her maternal uncle and exploited by Prof. Damle. Both the men do not want to carry further duties rather they practice the traditional approach of treating women as a sexual object.

The title of the play has different levels of inferences. Although it literally means the judge's order to maintain silence in the court-room, in the play the audience finds men not only silencing the woman and snatching her life. The very word 'silence' has a dual nature. When we consider as a noun, it means a lack of voice. As a verb means to suppress a voice and makes silence. In both of its versions, the word "silence" directs to patriarchy system that conditions woman the permanent toothless creature of the world. Tendulkar employs the word significantly. It has been reflected in the play as mute that imposes on a woman and it continues in the future also.

The play has three acts. As the play opens and we find a group of around ten people arrives at the village. These people have diverse backgrounds but all are members of 'The Sonar Moti Tenement (Bombay) Progressive Association (SMTPA)'. By enacting a mock trial, they try to create consciousness among people. This folk have reached to perform a mock trial protesting against President Johnson's production of atomic weapons. The action takes place in a hall near a village.

Vijay Tendulkar keeps the same setting and without lapsing much time throughout the play. Moreover, there are no scene divisions of the acts in the play. The first act provides the background information and Leela Benare's friendly nature to the reader-audience and introduces the salient attributes of different characters. To introduce the characters, Tendulkar proficiently uses routine talk and general gossip. The actual performance of the mock court is enacted in the evening so they have no alternative to spending the time except the 'game'.

An unmarried woman, Leela Benare, as a protagonist, plays the leading role, has been charged for having an illicit relationship with professor Damle and for infanticide is the central issue in the play. Sukhatme acts as a lawyer in the stage directions. The character, BaluRokde is a young and adopted boy. He is given shelter by the Kashikars, who provides food, cloth, and education him. Balu accompanies and takes orders from Kashikars. Ponkshe is a science student who has failed his intermediate examinations. He smokes a pipe and works as a clerk at the Central Telegraph office. Mrs. Kashikar and Mr. Kashikar is a married couple. Mr. Kashikar is the dominant husband and is very rude towards her, puts her down on every occasion. He is referred to as the chairman of the group by Benare. Karnik is an experimental theatre actor, habituated to chewing pan. Raghu Samant is a young, simple, innocent and friendly village boy.

Benare conveys Samant and the audience more about the other characters than she lets on about herself. WhenBenare is approached by Kashikarsheis quite unprepared as she comes out of the washroom, singing. Kashikar charges on her the crime of infanticide.The crime that despite being punishable by the law often surfaces in modern India. The first act comes to an end by making everyone serious and Benare in eye-catching condition. Suddenly, the play enters into a more real world of intrigue, suspicion, exploitation, crime, and recrimination. The first act concludes on a note of great anxiety.

While the first act is the exposition and allowed Benare to change our responses to all the other characters, Act II deals with new aspects of Benare's life. At the beginning of Act II, after a few false starts, humor and comic in nature, Benare declares untrue the charge against her, followed by the argument of the prosecution represented by Sukhatme. He puts forth the significance of motherhood. He also highlights the glorification as well as the adoration of the role of the mother in Indian culture. In addition, he quotes from the Sanskrit and reiterates the high status of the mother and the motherland, both of which supersede even that of heaven. Such magnificent elevations of women as mothers are part of the history of the nationalist movements. At that time we got to know that women's positions were fixed within the domestic procreative space around the perception of the motherland.

After declaring that the status of a mother is sanctified, the court proceeds to cross-examine Benare. The sudden shift comes at this juncture in the play. The mock trial shifts from the problem of infanticide to an investigation of Benare's personal affairs. All the characters appear to have a great deal of shocking pleasure and smugness who offer gossip details of their exchanges with Benare. The crux of the private secret slowly unveiling itself in Act II can be treated as the climax and finally made public in Act III. The private secret that how men view women and how the very mention of women conjures up certain stereotypical tasks and identities for a woman become obvious in Act III.

Act III is the most intense, serious, and comparatively longer than other acts. It seems to be the catastrophe of the play. The cross-examination is so firm and harsh that it exploits and hurts Benare.

She fails to answer any of the questions directed at her. The characters go on, and it thinks either this is a mock trial or a real court. The entire focus of Act III moves from an inquiry of the possibility of infanticide to a gradually constructed narrative of Benare's illicit relationship, her immorality, and the adenunciation of her very presence, which is seen as a canker in society.

Act III opens with breaking Benare's silence and communes it with the audience. Here the playwright artistically uses soliloquy to allow the expression of a woman's condition. Benare's soliloquy reveals her defiance and lets the audience view her situation from a different perspective. By using most of the male characters in the play, Tendulkar depicts the society of patriarchy, where a woman (Benare) not only gets secondary treatment but also exploits and harasses. Her words feel meaningless to deaf ears and frozen hearts and brains. The men are ready to hear what she wants to say. The judge of mock court, Kashikar, announces the verdict. Benare is seen as attempting to break all social codes and mores. She is accused of having committed a terrible crime, and she is ordered that the child in her womb will be destroyed. It proves the prejudiced mind of all male characters towards Leela Benare. The last scene on the stage is that of a Benare who takes great efforts to move but cannot. The play ends with a song of a grieving sparrow whose secure world has been demolished by predators.

A good woman is considered a good wife in Indian tradition. For example, Savitri and Satyavan, Nala and Damayanti, and Sita-Rama reflect the same. The women like Draupadi, Gandhari, Arundhati, and Ahilya are seen as symbols in the contexts of a traditional role as good wives. Why does a good woman have parameters and not for a good man? The answer is simple because males define parameters of good

and bad and women have no right to decide. Sita had to give the exam of her purity in the same way all men check her purity in the mock court in this play.

Modern writers have tried to change the traditional image of woman as seen in the myths and cultures. They began to portray women characters in a more realistic manner. We may find the traditional image of a woman in contemporary Indian literature has drastically changed. Vijay Tendulkar is a great illustration who has assigned different roles to women characters in his plays from different the roles enacted by women in traditional literature. The woman is no more, considered or portrayed as a feeble person, or falling at the feet of her husband or trying to please him every time. Tendulkar in *Kamala* and *Silence*! and Mahesh Dattani in *Dance Like* a *Man* and *Bravely Fought the Queen* portray new women in their plays. Carden has pointed out in this context is true to the protagonists of Tendulkar and Dattani:

> I want to have a part in creating a new society ... I want women to have something to say in their own lives...I have never reached my potential because of social conditions. I'm not going to get the reward; I have been crippled ...I want to see the kind of system that facilitates the use of potential. (12)

Vijay Tendulkar breaks the tradition by portraying 'a new woman' in his plays. The question put forth by Leela Benare in the play finds in all ages and societies. She is projected as a revolutionary woman who fights against the established patriarchal society. The playwright has not only revealed the new life of a new woman in his plays but also reflected feminism discourse, which has been governing the Indian scene for ages. However, his works grow out of his feminism and other political beliefs and ideologies.

The understanding of the centralized frame is vitally significant in this regard. Leela Benare, being self-conscious, tries to identify her as a valuable, self-dependent, and socially individual woman. She doesn't want to fit herself in patriarchal society and desires to create her world. But she forgets that she is the part and parcel of patriarchal traditional Indian society. The playwright understands the social issue of patriarchal taboos and exposes it in the play. Although most of Vijay Tendulkar's characters are built on the image of Indian women, Benare appears to be a modern and optimistic woman in the play when she sings a song:

The grass is green

The rose is red

The book is mine

Till I am dead. (Act 1.62)

The lines suggest the concept 'carpe diem' means to enjoy every moment in life without concern for the future. It also expresses her optimistic approach towards life as well as her free spirit. Her song also foretells the course of the play that she can have nothing that she can call her own; even an unborn child cannot take birth in this world due to the chain limited by patriarchal society on the name of morality. Her positive approach transforms into negative because a male-dominated world exists.

Vijay Tendulkar presents Leela Benare as a self-dependent working woman, and at the same time he exposes her unfortunate fate. She has two phases of her life in the play. The first is the pre-trial phase of her life, and the other is post-trial. At the very beginning of the play or in pre-trial, we find her as active, lively, energetic, and emotional and a self-assertive woman. She is seen as deeply committed to her profession and maintains her distinctive qualities and individuality.

We find a very interesting and detailed description of physical gestures in the conversion between Samant and Benare at the beginning. She holds her finger into her lips; that physical movement shows her free spirit nature. She tries to know Samant's personal life. His gesture indicates that he is a simple and shy person. With every inquiry, she wants to go closer to him. Why does Benare come close, and why teases Samant? Such actions exhibit her free, lively nature and a need for a man who can protect her from other men. While talking to Samant, she enjoys playing with his innocence and talks about her personality, her discipline, dedication, spontaneity, etc., but her words are like snatching blood and run away like a coward.

Here Samant tells the specialty of the entrance door. Sometimes the door becomes a trap due to some minor defect that cannot open from inside but only from outside. If someone closes the door strongly from inside, it will be stuck from outside, and the person is trapped inside. Actually, the door symbolizes transition and passageway from one place to another, but here Tendulkar uses the door artistically to show the trap for a woman.

The audience can realize that the door has some significant role, and Samant knows it, so he is not a newcomer. He narrated the story of how his finger got jammed in the stopper and how he had suffered. Again, Benare free spirit reveals:

> Goodness! I am feeling marvellous. I got down at the station with all the others, and suddenly, after many days, I felt wonderful! I felt even more wonderful coming here with you. I'm so glad the others fell behind! We rushed ahead, didn't we? Let's leave everyone behind, I thought, and go somewhere far, far away with you! (Act 2.55)

All statements of Leela Benare expose her personal life with zeal and aspiration, but the motives behind her queries remain unexposed only till the end of the play. She wants to enjoy life by forgetting reality, but members of a troop try to unravel her past in a mock trial. While uttering the above dialogues, she looks happy, cheerful, and innocent like a child. It clearly reflects that she is totally free and about to begin a new life in a new way. She seems to be free from all societal restrictions. We get to know that Benare is an impulsive and excitable young woman. So, in this respect, she is exposed to a New Woman in the Indian context.

She likes the company of Samant rather than the rest of the group. Her frank nature confuses Samant. He says "With me? ...you're very nice indeed. And shall I tell you something? You are a very pure and good person. I like you" (Act 1.55-56). It indicates that he is attracted by Benare. She also flirts with Samant. This juncture shows she is a caring woman of her desire and life. Miss Benare is conceived as an exact opposite to Kamala and Sarita presented in *KML*. Benare's introduction of other characters to Samant is rather sarcastic:

> There's Mrs. Hand-that- Rocks –the –Cradle. Excellent ...is! A real Hand-that-Rocks-the cradle type! BaluRokde. Who else? barristers' room at court, swatting ...precedents! us! (Puts an imaginary pipe in her mouth.) Hmm! Sci-en-list! Inter-failed! too. That means someone ...his book learning. But when there's a real-life problem, away he runs! Hideshis head. (Act 1. 59-60)

Here we see Leela Benare uses a satire to criticise others member of the group. Though it evokes humour, at the same time, it expresses internal anger inside her mind against the male-domination. Dharan comments, "The play is thus a satire on the conventions and hypocrisy of the middle class, male-dominated society which is concerned only with a farcical moral code. It is Benar's fear of such that makes her crave for marriage and forces her to beg the inferior men around, one after another, to marry in order to play the role of a father to her child" (56).

Being a school teacher and economically independent woman, she maintains her own philosophy of the emancipation and joyous living. Against patriarchal culture and myth of female subjugation, she declares her own individualism. She is a sprightly, rebellious and assertive as the heroines of Shakespeare's romantic comedies. She is sexually alive and needs to fulfill her desires and for that, she is not ashamed of her instinct. She defends her own nature:

> I'm the soul of seriousness! But I don't see why one should go around all thetime with a long face or a square face! ... We should play, we should sing! If we can and if they'll let us. We should dance too (Act 1.60)

It exposes that she hates to confirm herself with any established tradition and wants to have the full pleasure of life. As a teacher, she is more conscientious in her profession. She knows innocent the love and respect of all her pupils. So she utters:

> They are so much better than adults. At least they don't have that blind pride of thinking they know everything. There is no nonsense stuffed in their heads. They don't scratch you till you bleed, then runway like cowards. (Act 2.57)

Here we may understand Benare's feeling of resentment against the elder generation of her society. She feels comfortable in the company of students rather than the company of her generation. She knows that she is living in the society where a woman is treated inferior than man. In the company of elders, she acts as docile and dumb. Like others plays of Vijay Tendulkar here also we have the struggle of dominance and attainment of power.

Leela Benare seems to have full faith in the Darwinian dictum of "survival-of-the-fittest". Her struggle is not to attain dominance and power but to keep her own identity and resist another people's effort to dominate. Actually speaking, her fight is a fight for human survival. She asserts, "I say it from my own experience. Life is not meant for anyone else. It's your own life. It must be. It's a very, very important thing. Every movement, every bit of it is precious--- (Act 1.61).

On one hand, this interaction reveals her resistance against patriarchal culture, but on the other hand, there seems to be a fear of losing her job. The rhetorical outburst of Leela Benare expresses the contempt existing within her inner self, but at the same time, she tries to exhibit her confidence to identify her oppressor and resists the system of patriarchy. Her assertion indicates her non-conformity to the customs of the society,, like Sakharam Binder. He gets success to create his own world on his conditions by bringing women into his house. But Leela Benare fails and gets different treatment because she is a woman.

She leads full freedom of her life. But her free spirit suggests that she has broken some sorts of tradition by not taking heed of the dos and don'ts of society. We understand what she has done, as we are told that she unconsciously touches her abdomen and is alarmed when she becomes conscious of Samant's presence. These two actions are the symbolic predictions of the future course of action in the play. The twist of her mind is revealed through her dialogues and actions. The social consciousness reflects through her psychological stresses. Melaine Klein, Sigmund Freud's successor, admits:

> There no impulse, no instinctual urge or repose which is not experienced as unconscious fantasy ...Fantasy represents the particular content of urges or feeling (for example wishes, fears, anxieties, triumphs, love, or sorrow) dominating the mind at the moment. Unconscious fantasies are...an activity of the mind that occurs on deep unconscious levels and accompanies every impulse. (6)

Though some moral codes and rules are good to maintain society, they burn the natural desire of human beings. The society imposes its moral codes and restrictions on people, particularly women, and they become timid and passive. That is why the mock trial not only hurts much Benare but snatches her true nature. If she were not a woman, she would not have been exploited and hurt at all, or at least not in such a manner. It reveals gender discrimination. It also finds a distinction between how others in the group see her and how she sees herself. She cries out and confesses that she has committed a sin at the end of the play; these distinctions fade away. On the other hand, the authorities representing the law themselves are seen to be based on gender discrimination that indicates the violation of the law.

The mock trial in the play merely begins to pass the time till the show, but it is a very significant device so far in the play. On the surface, the members make a plan to kill the time and would enact an improvised trial, but actually they make a conspiracy against the unmarried girl, Leela Beenare. A rehearsal of a mock trial play is arranged, which is actually a "game" organized by the group. The real intention behind this conspiracy is to expose Benare's private life and her illicit relationship with Prof. Damale that results in her pregnancy. In such a roundabout way, she is exploited, harassed, and compelled to disclose her personal life before the court.

The question comes in my mind: why has Leela Benare been chosen for this trial court? Why not others? The answer may be simply that she has an illicit relationship with Prof. Damle and has the blame of infanticide, so it is an exciting issue to expose publically in court. It is apparently true,, but in reality, men like to tease a lonely woman and exploit her in a number of ways that proves in the play also.

At this juncture, the playwright skilfully employs the technique of play-within-play. It seems to be different from the conventional mousetrap method. We can take the example of Shakespeare's Hamlet to understand this concept. Play-within-play generally uses to disclose and entrap the guilty party or a single person who acts only as a spectator and not a part of the play performed within the play (Hamlet). The play-within-the-play here is not a small episode in its construction in the play, unlike Hamlet.

Excluding some tiny portions of its opening and the conclusion, the device comprises the whole of the play. Mousetrap also finds on different nature as far as the sympathies of the common reader or a viewer are concerned. Here, Leela Benare is not only entrapped in the game but also tormented and harassed by male dominance. This device not only exposes the personal relations of Benare but also unravels the mentality of these people. The playwright's foremost endeavor in this play is to depict the persecution of women in the so-called modern Indian society. By using the device on a different scale and of a different nature in silence *the Court is in session*, Vijay Tendulkar succeeds in exposing evil and harsh treatment to a woman given by patriarchal society.

Unfortunately, she becomes a victim of the sexual passion of Prof. Damle. She is conceived, and the pregnancy of an unmarried girl is generally believed to be a social sin in a patriarchal society. In order to save her own self-respect and the life of an unborn child, she makes the proposal of marriage with Rokde and Ponkshe, but her proposal is rejected by them. The unmarried mother is considered a sinner and treated badly in patriarchal society. Benare is also a victim of the same treatment and oppression. Hence, she has no supports and protections; Banare's counterparts successfully maneuver to exploit and victimize her, and she is forced to live a lonely, solitary life.

The double standard nature of society reflects in the play. It may forgive men who commit the worst sexual crimes, and it will blame women for violating so-called norms. Leela Benare strongly dissents patriarchal society and insists not only freedom but also the right over her body and to live the way she wants. Benare's lively nature and innocent beauty are twisted by these people who possess manly power ironically and thus exploit her in several times and several ways. However, she bears the violence and continues living joyfully.

She was seduced and sexually exploited in her teenageby her own uncle, who did not marry her and was supported by even her own mother. Benare not only overcomes this shock but also completes her education and becomes a teacher. She earns a good reputation as a teacher in the eyes of the pupils. That is the quality of 'new woman'. On the other hand, it feels and hurts male-domonated society. Sukhatme exposes in the court, "My information is that the accused attempted to suicide because of disappointment in love. She fell in love at the age of fifteen with her maternal uncle!" Sukhatme tries to prove how this woman is bad and concludes, "The present conduct of the accused is totally licentious... But it now seems that her past, too, is smeared in sin. This shows it as clear as daylight" (Act 3.111).

One by one the witnesses are summoned in the witness box to receive their opinion about the accusation of the case. They use the *Oxford English Dictionary* for taking the oath despite *Bhagwat Geeta* or *Bible.* Though it creates humour, it loses the seriousness of the court. It also degrades the law system. But Leela Benare is dealt with some degree of a serious criminal. The first witness is Ponkshe who gives a filthy statement about the character and conduct of Benare. He does not hesitate to give a disdainful statement, "To the public eye, she is unmarried" (Act 2.81).

Next Karnik appears in the witness box and speaks about motherhood without recognizing the gravity of the issue, "A mother is one who gives birth... Then she's a mother, of course. Who denied it? Who says only humans can be mothers and not dogs? "(Act 2.84).This exhortation shows various modes of humiliation and suppression of Benare. Even she is treated like a dog. After Karnik, Rokde is called as a witness. With the witness of Rokde, the mock-trial of Benare gradually shifts into the real experiences concerned with real life. He exposes the relation of Prof Damle and Benare and this revelation Benare become duller and more anxious. Sukhatme holds the chance and speaks about the incident of the visit of Benare to the Prof Damle'shouse.

His confession shows deep cruelty of men. This episode exposes the verbal cruelty more than physical cruelty. These comments make Benare powerless to restrain her suspended feelings. She maintains her strength and self-belief to hold her identity in patriarchy, yet having a realization of her weak position. She opposes, "There's no need at all to drag my private life into this.I can visit whom I like" (Act 2.87). Having understood the seriousness of this situation, Ponkshe comments casually on the motive of trial, "This is just game. A game that's all! Which of us is serious about the trial? It's fun". But Ponkshe declares unkindly, "only the accused is real" (Act 2.88).

The trial attains the goal, viz., the offender victim's penalty and the self-gratification and pleasure of victimizers. The target is the victim's innocence; spontaneity, independency, and brilliance, not only because of gender bias but also because these qualities of the woman make men feel mean and inferior. All the characters enact their roles with a naturalness that reveals patriarchal society and the genuineness of their prejudices against a woman who wants to be free and live as men living. She chooses the way to fulfill her sexual-emotional desire. That may not be a crime, but society considers the freedom of women a crime. Benare's persecutors might be natural in their conduct and ignorant in their cruelty, yet they are deceitfully vicious.

We can understand that even they use motherhood to disgrace Leela Benare Though a woman has one great superior quality and the right over the man, which is reproduction, yet this female right has been under the control of male authority. Sukhatme's assertion is a fine illustration:

> Motherhood is pure. Moreover, there is a great era, great nobility in our concept of motherhood. We have acknowledged a woman as the mother of mankind. Our culture ... She weaves a magic circle with her whole existence in order to protect and preserve her little ones. (Act 2.79)

This juncture exposesirony the view of people about motherhood. Undoubtedly, hereSukhatme idealizes motherhood without caring for society but at the same time, he abuses a mother's grace and her purity. The society is aware with the responsibility of the mother towards society but simultaneously it neglects to care for the dignity of the woman that shelters the child.

Here the judicial process aims at exposing the victim's sins. The prosecution of Benare exposes male's views towards woman. Itbecomes the most pleasurable thing to hold the mock-court since it satisfies the sadistic impulses of prosecutors. The more the victim (Benare) is distressed and anguished, the greater is their pleasure. Benare's defence and the refusal of the questions make them feel annoyed.They also think weak. Furthermore, they use male's authority and accuse her of messing up the "game".

> SUKHATME.Why are you so grave all of a sudden? After all, it's a game. Just a game, that's all. Why are you so serious?

BENARE .[Trying to laugh] : Who is serious? I'm absolutely – light –hearted. I just got a bit serious to create the right atmosphere.... (Act 2.75).

She is totally unaware about the conspiracy of those members. Tendulkar's use of the word "game" has great significance in that it exposes the organized conspiracy against the unmarried woman.

Tendulkar represents another female character in the play, Mrs. Kashikar. She passively accepts the role of a traditional wife and speaks only her husband speech. She has adopted her society's norms. Thus, she would see her own good only in her husband's good, even if her husband always snubs her. She may support her husband because she is not independent economically. It suggests that she is also a victim of patriarchy.

Mrs. Kashikar joins the men in attacking. She utilizes her womanhood in the act of dragging Benare into the witness box. She actually supports male dominance. Like traditional women, she follows patriarchal values in spite of their being unsafe and unsecure for women. It shows women are conditioned to accept and follow patriarchal norms. This may happen due to the fact that women urge for their survival to absorb, observe, and propagate patriarchal culture. Mrs. Kashikar, in spite of being a woman, doesn't understand and support Benare, which represents the traditional jealousy existing among women and joins with the rest of the people. Hence, the critics of feminism realize the problem and declare that women are real enemies of women. She pitilessly criticizes Benare for remaining unmarried:

> That's what happens these days when you get everything without marrying. They just want comfort. They couldn't care less about responsibility! ... It's the sly new fashion of women earning that makes everything go wrong. That's how promiscuity has spread throughout our society. (Act 3. 99-100)

The dialogue expresses her rage for the new and unconventional woman. While Mrs. Kashikar is a woman herself but she is also a part of the patriarchal system. She is a dependent wife who is rebuked by her husband every other time. She has passively accepted male domination.

Mrs. Kashikar further says, "It's the sly new fashion of woman earning that makes everything go wrong.That's how promiscuity has spread throughout the society" (Act 3.100). It seems that she feels jealousy because Benare is an economically independent woman. Mrs. Kashikar also exposes the traditional view of patriarchy about matrimony in which woman is exploited and becomes an integrated part of her husband.

MRS KASHIKAR:I don't think so. We see too many such examples.

SUKHATME: Forget about the others. Have you any proof where Miss Benare is concerned? Any proof? Tell me if you.

MRS KASHIKAR: What better proof? Just look at the way she behaves. I don't like to say anything since she's one of us. Should there be no limit to how freely a woman can behave with a man? ...day in and day out! (Act 3.100)

Another fact about Mrs. Kashikar that she can't bear any children is torture enough in Indian society. The exploiter is, in turn, the exploited too in this way. Tendulkar has dexterously portrayed the characters in the play. He portrays the agents of patriarchy as embodiments of hypocrisy, selfishness, and treachery. The male characters like Damle, Kashikar, Sukhatme, Ponkshe, Karnik and particularly absent character, Prof. Damle whose words, behaviour and deeds expose their inherent wickedness and hypocrisy are all set to impose silence upon the independent woman.

The idea of mock-trial is significant where a woman is exposed. So, Sukhatme becomes curious about the presence of the woman in the law court. Sukhatm says "There is not much difference between one trial and another. But when there's a woman in the dock, the case does have a different complexion, that's true that is my experience well, Mr. Karnik" (Act 1.73). The statement indicates how the trial, for whom and why is organized. It also shows the hidden motives of the people. The purpose of mock-trial shifts from a rehearsal to 'a game of humiliation', where a woman is exploited and brutalized by males. Tendulkar expertly manifests woman's torment in a mock court. Similarly, suffering and sorrow of Kamala take place at Press conference that creates greater sensations in the play *Kamala.*

Finding Benare in the witness box, Sukhatme wears his gown and advises Mr. Kashikar to put his gown on. Sukhatme makes well propaganda of her life with his all cruelty and wretchedness. He asks all the questions that are related to her personal life. The public exposition of personal life concerns her profession, age, love affair, and marital status. It shows the gender consciousness and the hypocrisy and hollowness of existing in these male counterparts.

The lawyer puts a very disgraceful question before the court, "Can you tell the court how you came to stay unmarried to such a mature... How many chances of marriage have you had so far in your life? And how did you miss them" (Act 3.98). Therefore, we find that women avoid launching a complaint against such men who exploit, tease, harass, and forcefully sex them in reality.

Consider the Vishaka case; that would help to understand the law system and judiciary process. The case relates to a woman, Bhanwari Devi, who worked for an NGO. She tried to stop child marriage in the remote village of Rajasthan state. Her family is opposed to such great work. One day members of the groom and bride came to her house and gang-raped her, in the witness of her husband, who was helpless. She ran for justice from one police station to another, but she failed to avail justice. At last, she knocked on the doors of the court. Her efforts for justice gave birth to a new concept sexual harassment of women at the workplace.

Tendulkar efficiently exposes the patriarchal society and examines the mechanism of power relations in society with the intention of shattering them down. The court is considered the supreme authority, and it functions to protect human rights and announce verdicts without bias. But here we find the judicial machinery fails in executing its duty and responsibility and verdicts with bias.

The group of members makes use of the court for their pleasure. We experience the process of the court exploiting, castigating, and penalizing a woman. Once hounded by every member of the theater group, Benare falls to the pattern of the centuries of the learned unconscious and loses her independent spirit. She begins to justify her conduct rather than attacking those vultures of patriarchy. In her attempt to justify her character, she feeds and creates fun for her miserable self. Describing Leela Benare's character, Arundhati Banerjee remarks:

> Leela Benare, the central character of the play is the only exception. Possessing a natural lust for life and spontaneous *joie se vivre* fraught with frustrations and repressed desires. She ignores social norms and dictates. Being different from others, she is easily isolated and made the victim of a cruel game, cunningly planned by her co-actors. (viii)

She is obliged to feel handicapped only because she is a woman.A woman has always been the subaltern across cultural boundaries. Men need her, praise her, love her, adore her and write about her; but they do purposefully to their own lives. In patriarchal society, male privilege is marked as having control over protection and representation of pleasure. Cultural representations have been made to have room for male preferences and patterns of gratification. Women's rights and pleasures have been reduced in importance to implant morality.

It is a common experience that men insult women unnecessarily in a male-dominated society. They pass insulting remarks and it results in the degradation of women. So the Indian government passed the law against such incidents under section 294, which sentences a man found guilty. In the play, a number of insulting comments are made by male characters, especially on Miss Leela Benare. For example, 'she runs after men too much', 'the prisoner sometimes acts as if she were off her head,' 'that is there's sometimes no sense at all in her action.' All these comments humiliate and blacken Miss Leela Benare's character. In addition, Rokade only sees Miss Leela Benare in Professor Damale's house and this is enough for him to show and propagate a seducer woman. Thus, feminine stereotype thinking works against women

The psychological analysis of the characters reveals why they behave and treat Benare in an exploitative way. The first and foremost reason is obvious: they reveal the inner core of their mind that, being men, they should rule over the woman. Secondly, she is perfect in her professional career and an economically independent woman. Thirdly, they have to convict Benare anyhow for conceiving a child out of wedlock. Fourthly, it is their failures in life. Therefore, they disturb Benare in a callous and pitiless manner. Actually, characters like Kashikars, BaluRokde, Sukhatme, Ponkshe, and Karnik are incompetent and dissatisfied, but they are men of society.

Their words and actions indicate that they are dissatisfied, hung up, scheming, and even deceitful. It is also obvious that they have turned to the theater to fulfill their personal failures. They can arrange the conspiracy against each other. In other words, to expect them to be refined, honest, and kind is perhaps next to impossible. The characters are actually feeble, but still, they attempt to exercise their manly power on Benare. In her own way, Benare tries to resist by making fun of the characters' personal failures and thus belittle their authority. Kashikar's shocking and scornful opinion proves his traditional mind:

> KASHIKAR.What I say is, our society should revive the old custom of child marriage. Marry off the girls before puberty. All this promiscuity will come to a full stop. If anyone has ruined our society it's Agarkar and Dhondo Keshav Karve.
>
> SUKHATME.[With a lawyerlike bow]: Yes, milord. (Act 3.98)

Kashikar's remark not only insults social reformers but also shows his irrational mind. In history, there were some customs of polygamy, the denial of women's right over property, sati Pratha, and child marriage. All these practices made women weak and inferior in many respects. The result of it was the social movements for reforms in those evils which were prevalent in the society. Some social reformers and leaders like Raj ram Mohan Roy, Agarkar, and Dhondo Keshav Karve came ahead, fought against such customs and changed child marriage. Sukhatme's accusation is equally degrading Benare:

> Her conduct has blackened all social and moral values. The accused ispublic enemy number one. If such socially destructive tendencies are encouraged to flourish, this country and its culture will be totally destroyed. (Act 3.114-15)

Thus, the self-proclaimed 'fathers' of society pronounce verdict on the behavior of woman and consequently curb her freedom. The frustrated male members of a society attempt to suppress women to exercise their power and superiority in the social hierarchy. "But the child in your womb shall be destroyed" (Act 3.119). They praise motherhood pompously but they are not ready to accept an infant in the womb of Benare. This is pinpointed instance of sham and double- standard prevalent in society. Benare is stigmatized and fired from her job. But being a male, Prof. Damle escapes from all the suffering.

Tendulkar presents how the urban middle-class society holds a mock trial in the form of a law court to enslave fair sex by managing a hypocritical moral code. It also reveals how particular men silence a woman for their interests and intentions in the name of morality. Though Benare is shown as the cheerful and talkative lady at the beginning of the play, yet silence is imposed on her. The forced silence later makes her entirely dumb. Benare desperately fights her single-handed battle and shouts that her path of life and her choices are her own, but her natural voice is silenced by the destructive agents of patriarchal society.

She longs to displace and uproot the patriarchal hierarchy and decides not to pay any attention to what society says of women. Instead, she would live her life in a manner she desires. She has learned from life that when one dies, only that person dies; no one else is willing to give a little of their lives to that person.

Without asking a single question to Prof. Damle, the court pronounces the verdict on Benare and punishes her. It shows the patriarchal approach of men who support a man who is really accused of physical exploitation of Benare. The inside and the outside are thus witnessed as only convenient distinctions, behind which deeper patriarchal society stands. The play reveals the construction of a woman's prejudice under the twin discourses of patriarchy and individualism. Whereas patriarchy rules over women, oppresses and silences a woman into subjugation, and individualism only ignites her challenge and opposes patriarchal norms.

Before passing the final verdict on her, Benare is given ten seconds to defend her case. The motionless Benare stands up erect and says, "Yes, I have a lot to say" (Act 3.116). Then follows a long monologue in which Benare expresses her zest for life and tells how she is deprived of her wishes:

> My life was a burden to me. (Heaving a great sigh) But when you can't lose it, you realize the value of it... There's great joy in a suicide that's failed. It's greater even than the pain of living... I swallowed that poison, but didn't even let a drop of it touch them! ... I cried inside, and I made them laugh. I was cracking up with despair, and I taught them hope. (Act 3.116-17)

> Furthermore, she launches her disdainful attack against patriarchy in this monologue:

> These are the mortal remains of some cultured men of the twentieth century. See their faces—how ferocious they look! Their lips are full of lovely worn-out phrases! And their bellies are full of unsatisfied desires. (Act 3.117)

In the final verdict, Benare finds 'criminals and sinners' and the court orders that she should live but the child in her womb should be destroyed. Writing in pain, Benare at first strongly resists, and then stifled sobs come from her. L. Rahman in his book Tendulkar's 'Silence! The Court is in Session's comments, "Once Benare finds her voice couched in questioned language does make no truth-effect, she begins to sob with the idea in mind that though the field be lost, all is not lost; she has a mind which remains and will remain unconquered by the oppressive patriarchal ideology" (22).

The play was written under great pressure due to the performance date. The playwright completed the play just a few days ahead of the show. But Arvind Deshpande, the director, interfered and insisted that it was imperfect without a statement by Benare at the end. He gave the reason that she couldn't simply accept the terrible verdict pronounced against her and say nothing in her own defense. Initially, the playwright was against such monologue or statement. Tendulkar gives a reason: Benare would never make it, and the impact of the brutal verdict would be reduced by its presence. But, finally, however, Deshpande convinced Tendulkar, and the latter wrote the speech.

Instead of a speech, Tendulkar spared ten minutes to expose her suppressed anger and frustration against the well-structured mechanism of a patriarchal society where hardly a woman possesses her existence and own voice. Sulabha Deshpande argues that the monologue is so full of Benare's internal turbulence, her world view, her rebelliousness, her rage against a society that is happy to live in a rut without aim or purpose, her bitterness at the harassment she has suffered at its hands. She says,

"The resulting helplessness, her yearning for the laughing, romping, dancing life that is soon to be hers, her determination to bear it" (Mulye 16).

The soliloquy throws light on the oppressive system of patriarchal society. We know that women have been suffered for centuries. Their voice has always remained suppressed by male counterparts or by the patriarchal society. The same we find in the life of Benare. First, she has been sexually exploited by her maternal uncle and later by Prof Damle. It clearly shows the double-slandered nature of the people. They are ready to enjoy sex but they reject the responsibility. Arundhati Banerjee asserts:

> Leela Benare'sdefense of herself against the onslaught of the upholders of social norms in a long soliloquy has become famous in the history of contemporary Marathi theatre. It is important to note here that Tendulkar leaves us in doubt as to whether or not Benare at all delivers the soliloquy, thus, suggesting that in all probability what she has to say for herself is swallowed up by the silence imposed upon her by the authorities. In fact, during the court proceedings, on several occasions, her objections and protestations are drowned by the judge's cry of silence and the banging of the gravel. (ix)

Tendulkar felt a requirement to include a woman voice on the issue that was concerned with woman's dignity and self-respect after the suggestions and discussion with the director Arvind Deshpande and the Marathi actress Sulbha Deshpande, When Tendulkar is ready to compose the monologue for Benare, he becomes feminist. Tendulkaradmits:

> She suggested that the central character of the play Miss Benare must open up somewhere, especially at the end of the last act. She could express her pent up feelings by way of monologue. Without Benare's

> articulation, the play would remain less communicative ... I was compelled to write. So I made Benare fly into fantasy and made her recite a prolonged monologue.(Agrawal 64)

Including this self –a reflection of Benare, Tendulkar attempts to construct the vision of female voice gender-based social system of patriarchy. If He had not introduced the soliloquy of Benare, the playwright would have been called anti-feminist. He artistically portrays the feminine issue in a male-dominated society and gives outlet in the soliloquy. There is no torment for the Alecs and Prof. Damle because of men and every time Tess and Miss Benare have to prove their purity in this male dominated world.

As we know thatmonologue of Benare has a strong impact and distinctiveness of the play, words are carefully used, and it reveals obscurities and hints of Benare's suppressed emotions and at the same time she challenges the society. There is always criticism about whether Benare would have exposed her suppression in the presence of the people who would be the last to understand her feelings. The monologue is a lampoon that presents the irony, sorrow in the Indian society.

> Arundhati Banerjee compares it with Nora's declaration in Ibsen's A Doll's House. She says that Benare's monologue is reminiscent of Nora's declaration of independence but lacks the note of protest that characterizes the speech of Ibsen's heroine. It is more a self-justification than an attack on society's hypocrisies. It is poignant, sensitive and highlights the vulnerability of women in our society. (Banerjee 569)

Though Benare is provided with a long monologue, it is evident that nobody is on the stage and no one hears her. Though she is educated and articulate like Sarita in Kamala, she is unable to present her feelings to her prosecutors. The child in her womb, her attempts at suicide, snatching her job demonstrates Benare's oppression in the male-dominated world.

During mock-trial Benare remains completely silent due to the dissection of her personal life by her fellow actors. Even if she tries to speak, she is silenced by them. The playwright exposes two symbols. One is Benare who wants to live with free nature without any limitations and restrains and the second symbol is deaf ears of society which never admits her freedom in a patriarchal society. Her reply falls on deaf ears of the patriarchal system, but she exposes her internal voice. It suggests tendulkar's inclinations towards feminism. Benare has no alternative without accepting the Court's verdict and she must have to live in the social structure of patriarchy. Tendulkar clearly depicts about Benare's condition in his stage directions at the end of the play "Benare feebly stirs a little... then gives up the efforts..."(Act 3.120). Director's point of view about this monologue can be justified through a simple argument made by Sulabha Deshpande who argues:

> The play would have completely collapsed if the audience had felt, even for one moment, that the punishment Benare was awarded was justified since she had committed the "crimes' of falling in love with her uncle and attempting suicide at the age of fourteen, and, conducting an 'illicit' relationship with a married man, insisting on having his illegitimate baby and still asking to be permitted to face her impressionable students at school as if she had done no wrong. (Mulye 16)

The play reflected that how a woman was transformed from her true nature to the pathetic position of women in the male-dominated Indian world. All philanthropic assumptions of human nature have been thoroughly butchered. In the opinion of Shubha Tiwari, "the play poignantly portrays the plight, the ponderings, predicaments, and problems of a middle-class Indian woman. Society as a force is hostile to individual instincts as well as dignity. The very system of justice is gender biased"(35).

Being interested in acting of drama, Benare becomes a member of drama troupe of amateur artists. But she fails to understand the mentality of the people. Although men of this group fail in their actual life, they pass in mock-trial to exploit a woman. So, they try to gratify their unfulfilled wishes through drama. Tendulkar provides an interesting contrast in every character.

Benare, the protagonist is a successful character in her personal life, but the society compels her to commit suicide means she is also a failure in the code and conduct of patriarchal society. Rokde is a lawyer but no client comes to near him and he is going to play the role of the lawyer in the mock trial. Ponkshe who failed in intermediate is going to play a scientist in the mock trial. Prof. Damle who is absent for mock trial but Tendulkar explores his characteristics through dialogues of other people. We can see that Prof. Damle is a scholar and lover of books but escapes when the real problem arises. It means everyone is a failure in one sense or the other in their personal lives still they are men armed with the privilege of male-world order to rule over women and they successfully impose their power on a woman by becoming a victim.

As we can see, Leela Benare has an instinctual will to lead a free life. During the first half of the play, she is bold, strong and self-assertive and wants to set her own identity. She can outsmart them. Her voice is full of courage and is not throttled by anybody. But the latter half of the play reveals male-dominated society and their organized conspiracy against a woman in the mock-trial. Where she is exploited and seems to be helpless and passive. Here is not the problem of Benare, single woman who is trapped in this world of organized conspiracy but the whole female race in this country. It shows our hypocrisy, our double standards, regarding men and women.

Tendulkar renders the exploitation of a woman and the cruelty of the people that impose the mechanization of power. Benare frightens away the other characters when they enter the Village Hall. She mocks at Ponkshe and she laughs at Rokde. She is the "soul of seriousness but she never goes around with a long face". Even innocent Samantcomplements, "Miss Benare is really amazing", "this lady behaved in a most exemplary manner", she's a very nice lady".

As a teacher, she is known for her punctuality. She has never given "a bit of room for disapproval" She says: "I don't give an inch of it to anyone". Her class is scared of her, yet she is adored. She would spend "the last drop of her blood in teachingthem".The other teachers as well as the Principal are jealous of her. She is a keen observer. She can see how Mr. and Mrs. Kashikar have sheltered Rokde in order to flee from the sordidness of their lives and have made "a slave" of him. She is rebellious.

The Exploitation of a Woman

Friedrich Engels explored the exploitation of women in his well-known book. *The Origin of the Family and Private Property and the State.* He further stated that though there was a gender division of labor, there existed a basic equality between men and women in ancient times. Men were basically hunters responsible for production, while women were responsible for reproduction. So, they had a high social status since reproduction was a crucial issue. But in reality, men controlled it.

Like two sides of one coin, there is a strong connection between patriarchal culture and the exploitation of women. Therefore, radical feminists strongly oppose patriarchal culture. The fact cannot be denied that women have been the victims of exploitation by men for a long time. They are exploited in different fields, both physically and mentally. There are several causes of sexual as well as moral abuse that are very often highlighted by the media, and a lot of those too remain unexplored. Although the malpractices to women are age-old, while identifying its key reasons, it is realized that the long-run supremacy of male over female in all respects in the patriarchal society in India is highly responsible for creating hurdles in the process of the empowerment of women. Consequently, they are being trafficked for sex, abused at workplaces, and tortured in family and society. Her status as a woman is outshined by her identity as a mother, a sister, a wife, or a daughter. Women continue to be subjected to harassment over the entire life cycle, irrespective of their class, caste, and educational status.

The patriarchy has a rigid social system, which is very complex and makes women suffer a great deal. The notable critics Sujata and Gokulwani observe, "Patriarchy has always hindered women from exercising their power and releases themselves off the control over them. The culture of most of the countries is patriarchal, and a woman is in a constant fight for rights" (48).

The ruminations made by Vijay Tendulkar are essentially true, realistic, and fearless. Although Tendulkar has not given the solution to such social problems, yet his major works blow sirens against this patriarchal system and demand social justice for women. The patriarchy and women's exploitation highlighted by Vijay Tendulkar in this play is an outcome of his serious investigation made into a systematic mode.

Tendulkar exposes the vices and weakness of women characters. That is why he was charged with anti-woman. Tendulkar explained his stand in an interview.

> When I show the struggle of a woman, it is not one woman's fight. The individual must have name and identity and caste and background to be credible, but she is not just a woman on stage, in particular play. I am, in writing of her situation, showing that the possibility of a struggle against it exists...By not giving a solution, I leave possibilities open, for whatever course the change may take. When the members of my audience go home and chew on the situation, they might be able to see their daughter or sister in the women's position and come up with a way of changing the situation for advantage. (Wadikar 72)

The view of Tendulkar proves that he is a feminist. He opposes patriarchy and deals with female's issues poignantly. He exposes whatever around us. He is very conscious that women's progress is hindered by the patriarchal attitude of men and portrays the same condition in the play with two female characters. But Leela Benare actively revolts against the culture while Miss Kashikar passively accepts the role of wife and always finds with her husband.

The playwright has noted that his choices were dictated by feminist choices which he has perceived in his major works. His *Silence! The court is in Session* reflects endlessness of the game of a woman's exploitation. It reveals how a character specifically a woman has been harassed and exploited. Smita Paul in her book *Theatre of Power* states that:

> The women characters in Tendulkar's theatre undergo a series of sufferings and tortures as the victims of the hegemonic power structure. In the male-dominated theatre-world, they are constantly being 'othered'. In Silence! The focal point of interest lies in the struggle between women like Benare and her antagonists headed by the orthodox Kashikar and his associates. (61)

There are latent hints of her suppressed sufferings in her dialogues throughout the play. At the very beginning of the play, we find Benare as aenergetic, emotional but a self-assertive woman. She is deeply committed to her profession. But there are latent hints of her suppressed sufferings. "There is a great joy in a suicide that's failed. It is greater even than the pain of living" (Act 3.116). Here Benare knows the futility of the existence of the woman in a patriarchal society which suppresses the desire of a woman.

Benare is trapped in a web of multiple discourses pulling and tearing her apart. Similarly, the play also looks into the bias of the oppressors as to what makes them so cruel, intolerant, and unreasonable. It is an indication of a male's power. Therefore, M. SaratBabu says, "The play, Silence! *The Court is in session and* exposes the inhuman violence in its verbal form of the patriarchal society against women»(6). The statement clearly indicates that there is still the existence of patriarchy, and that imposes silence on women. Society rarely consents to fair sex to live free. Every day we talk about women's empowerment and their rights. Still, people are reluctant to give women their rights and freedom among many sections of the country.

The critics and the scholars may express different opinions about the technical aspects of the play, but all agree on the point of exploitation of women as the central idea because of a male-dominated society. In my perspective, Benare becomes a victim of patriarchal society and her exploitation through the game planned by men. The central idea is all about the issue of gender. Rousseau asserts, "Man is born free, but he is everywhere in chains." It is an admitted fact that we are born as human beings, but gender-based socialization basically divides us into male and female fragments.

Finally, she declares in a depressed mind, "Milord, life is a very dreadful thing. Life must be hanged; Life is not worthy to life.' Hold an inquiry against life. Sack it from its job! But why?" (Act 3.118). She shows her fury against the decision of the authority who determines the course of life of Benare either she will live with her child or not. She confesses her relationship with her uncle. But it is not meant for her guilty

Though it is an improvised mock trial on the surface level, the game has begun internally. It is the game of silence women and its core is cruelty and brutality. People like Kashikar, Sukhatme, Ponkshe, Rokde, Karnik and Prof. Damle represent the herd instincts of the failed and the powerless who try to wind up their flaws and failure under the guise of morality. It is the pseudo-morality which enslaves a woman who has her own desires.

The case is taken on the charge of infanticide in the mock –trial. The accused has brutally been tortured physically, mentally and emotionally at the floor of the court. The lawyer exposes the positions of the persons like Benare who has broken the traditions of society. Mr. Kashikar verdicts:

> No memento of your sin should remain for future generations. Therefore, this court hereby sentences that you shall live. But the child in your womb shall be destroyed. (Act 3.119)

On this verdict, Benare sits down with half fainting. There is no possibility to hear the voice of the woman in the gender discrimination system. Her identity becomes more significant of a butchered sparrow or a dolled parrot. She sings a poignant song at the end of the play that intensifies the emotional effect of the play. She sings:

The parrot to the sparrow said,

'Why! Oh, why are your eyes so red?

Oh! , my friend, what shall I say?

Someone has stolen my nest away.'

Sparrow, sparrow, poor little sparrow. (Act 3.121)

The heart rendering story of sparrow and crow is very appropriate to expose the story of Miss Leela Benare. The cry of a sparrow is the loss of her identity and the anguish of Benare. The story reminds us of the struggles of women like Sita in the great epic Ramayana and Tess in Hardy's novel *Tess of D'Urbervilles*. Sita had to suffer the ordeal of fire to prove her purity, and Tess sustains those high feminine virtues but a rigid social system that cannot permit spaces for her. Here the organized conspiracy in the form of mock court also attempts to unravel Benare, but the people enable her to subdue her courage to fight for her identity.

Tendulkar puts forth the helpless condition of women in the Indian context. Benare's desperate situation exposes the inhuman violence lurking beneath the respectable exterior of Indian society, especially the middle class. The presentation of a serious issue in a light comic way is effective in unfolding the evil existing in the human mind and also in the structure of patriarchy.

The audience understands here how the masks of gentility and civilization are uncovered from the faces of Sukhatme, Karnik, Ponkshe, Rokde, and the Kashikar couple. They are overwhelmingly portrayed as predatory vultures—as 'gidhare' waiting to pounce upon their victim, an individual who has the intellectual ability and moral courage to attain success and to fulfill her private desires. The play can thus be investigated to disclose the construction of a woman's prejudice under both discourses of patriarchy and individualism.

Thus, the play has dealt with the erroneous practices of patriarchal society. The play finely demonstrates that the patriarchal ideology is intended in such a way that traps and exploits women. Women are unable to find a path where they may be considered as human beings. Women are treated as commodities for sensual pleasure. Socializations and institutes are responsible for making women's lives pathetic. The court makes women's lives more miserable, and the marriage institute questions women only.

By providing such an infanticide issue, Tendulkar appeals to us to view critically the mindset of a society that constitutes two sets of rules, one for men and another for women. We are made aware of the authority wielded by the powerful and the helplessness of the small individuals who are trapped within the snare of primitive social mores and constraints

In the patriarchy, the educational institute does injustice to women. One finds the view of Simon de Beauvoir justified when she notes that "... her wings are cut, and then she is blamed for not knowing how to fly" (Beauvoir 660). The patriarchal culture or society treats a woman in the same way, which reflects in the play. The second act deals with cutting the wings of Benare, and in the third act everybody talks that she is unable to fly in this world. In short, the play is keenly representative of the women's suffering in patriarchal culture. If we want to change patriarchal society, only the change of mindset will bring a new system.

The crucial role played by literature has highlighted the issue. By creating a real-life situation and giving us all the points of view through a host of characters, the playwright expects us to contemplate the issue. Benare's story ends sadly, but it has definitely alerted us to women's weakness and exploitation in a patriarchal society.

Works Cited

Agrawal, Beena. *Dramatic World of Vijay Tendulkar Exploration andExperimentations*. Jaipur: Aadi publications, 2012. Print.

Babu, M Sarat."Introduction", *Vijay Tendulkar's GHASHIRAM KOTWAL', AReader's Companion*. New Delhi: Asia Book Club, 2003. Print.

Banerjee, Arundhati, "Introduction", *Five Plays of Vijay Tendulkar*. Bombay: OUP, 1992: iii Print.

---. Appendix I. "Note on Kamala, Silence! The Court is in Session, Sakharam Binder, The Vultures, Encounter in Umbugland". *Collected Plays in Translation* .NewDelhi: OUP. 2003. Print.

Carden, Maren Lockwood. *The New Feminist Movement*. New York:Russel Sage Foundation, 1974. Print.

De Beauvoir, Simone *The Second Sex*. Trans. Constance Borde and Sheila Malovany London: Vintage Books, 2011.Print.

Durrant, Will.*The Story of Civilization* Part I .New York: Simon & Schuster, 1963. Print.

Gokhale, Shanta. "Tendulkar on His Own Terms", Vijay Tendulkar inconversation withShanta Gokhale, *KATHA* publication, New Delhi: 2001. Print.

Heywood, Andrew, *Political Ideologies*, Pal grave Macmillan, 2003, Print.

Jain, Jasbir. "Positioning the 'Post' in Post-Feminism: Reworking of Strategies?" Ed.Jasbir Jain, Avadhesh Kumar Singh. *Indian Feminisms.* New Delhi: Creative Books, 2001.Print.

Iyer, N. Sharda. Musings on Indian Writing in English. Vol.3. New Delhi: Samp& Sons, 2007. Print.

Klein, M. *Our Adult World and its Roots in Infancy.*London .1960.Quoted in *The Psychology of Tragic Drama (*ed.) Patrick Roberts.Routledge and KeganPaul, 1975.Print.

Mulye, Pradip, Rajiv Naik, and Vijay Tapas, Eds. *Ten Ani Amhi,* Mumbai:AwishkarPrakashan, 1992. Print.

Paul, Smita. *Theatre of Power,* Kolkata: Books Way Publishers & Distributors,2010.Print.

Rahman, L. (2010). "Tendulkar's 'Silence! The Court is in Session": *A Study inPerspectives.* Kolkata: Books Way Publishers &Distributors.2010.Print.

Sujatha K.R., and Gokilavani, S. *Feminine Aesthetics of Indian Women Writers.*Delhi: Regal Publications, 2011. Print.

Sathe, Dr.Makarand."Tendulkar and violence – Then and Now" in a documentary*Interview of Vijay Tendulkar.* Print.

Tendulkar, Vijay. *Five Play.* Silence! The Court is in Session. Trans. Priya Adarkar.New Delhi: OUP, 1974.pp. 55-121. Print.

Thankamma, Catherine. "Women that Patriarchy Created: The Plays of VijayTendulkar, Mahesh Dattani and Mahasweta Devi." *Vijay Tendulkar's Plays: AnAnthology of Recent Criticism.*Ed.V.M. Madge. New Delhi: PencraftInternational, 2007. Print.

Tiwari, Subha. "Silence! The Court is in Session: A strong Social Commentary"*Contemporary of Indian Dramatists.* Ed. Shubha Tiwari. New Delhi: AtlanticPublisher, 2007.Print.

Wadikar, Shailaja B.*Vijay Tendulkar A Pioneer Playwright.* New Delhi: AtlanticPublisher, 2008.Print.

Kamala: The Liberation of Women

Feminism means the belief and aim that women should have the same rights and opportunities as men and the tireless effort to achieve this aim. It intends to liberate women from various manifestations of gender-based exploitation and discrimination. The liberation of women is essential to making progress in the entire world. The liberation of women is the cornerstone of feminism. We can find many approaches towards feminism: liberal feminism, Marxist feminism, psychoanalytical, postcolonial, multiculturalism, and radical feminism. Liberal feminists advocate for equal rights and privileges for all citizens. The eighteenth-century enlightenment projects promotion of universal liberty and equality. If both sexes have the same power of reason, then liberty and equality should get to women also.

Here is an attempt to critically analyze Vijay Tendulkar's play, *Kamala*. The liberation of women is one more element of feminist that appears on a deep level and is not found on a surface level in this play. Tendulkar admits the law of nature that every woman is an individual with a distinctive identity of her own, and her identity cannot be crushed and crippled in the male-dominated world. We should treat them as human beings. Therefore, the playwright explores women's liberation from his perspective to redefine themselves and to make a protest against the humiliations and cruelty done to them. Tendulkar believes that women can shift their positions from suppression to objection' and 'objection to liberation.'

Feminism is a worldwide phenomenon. It is a global and revolutionary ideology. It is a socio-cultural movement that aims at the freedom of women from male supremacy in the patriarchal society.The women's liberation movement is a solemn reform movement. It aims at uplifting women in society. The first voice in favor of women's rights was raised by

Mary Wollstonecraft in her major literary work. *A Vindication of the Rights of Women (*1972). She strongly demanded equal opportunities for women in the respects of education, economics, and politics.She further argued that women should be allowed the same rights and privileges as men on the basic grounds that they too were human beings. John Stuart Mill is also a strong male adherent of women‘s liberation. He showed serious concern about women's oppression in his book *The Subjugation of Women (1859).* He felt the dire need for education to improve the condition of women and condemned women oppression as domestic slavery.

The first major wave of feminism came in the nineteenth century as a suffragette movement. The second wave occurred in the 1960s on a global scale. Liberation is concerned with human civil rights. The liberation of women means the progress towards equal rights, which it achieves through various means. Gradual reforms and social reformation are not enough to get equality for women. As we know, sex is a biological difference like reproductive roles, etc., while gender is constructed culturally and socially that makes the division between masculinity and femininity and ideas of their abilities. According to Aristotle "Women are primarily associated with home and man with the outside world. A woman is to man as a slave to the master, the barbarian to the Greek. A woman is an unfinished man, left standing on a lower step in the scale of development" (Durant107).

We are living in the 21st century, but the condition and status of women are inferior to men. They are far away from progress. The male-dominated world considers still weaker sex, and the male society exploits whether she is educated, illiterate, or she may be working outside the house. She is never given her chance to express her thoughts and feelings in or outside the house by the male-dominated society. Her role is constrained to cook, to rear the children, and to be obedient to her husband within the house as an ideal housewife. Tendulkar explores a confine-like situation at home and this fact of women folk in this play.

In reality, there are certain jobs that are assigned to women, such as cooking, serving food, cleaning the house, and very important childbearing. Men cannot perform such works, and there are certain works that men have to do. A good example is driving; women can drive in the west, but they cannot drive in Saudi Arabia.

The enlightened ideas of the French Revolution have brought significant changes in the status of women. The background of fraternity, equality, and liberty, along with the liberal philosophy of individualism, made women more conscious of the fact that it is the social processes that determine her life. This added to an intense dislike among women for these so-called customs, traditions, and cultures.

Liberal feminists strongly consider the liberation of women and accept the basic structure of society, but at the same time they seek to expand the rights and opportunities of women. It also supports equal rights and opposes prejudice and discrimination that hamper the ambitions of women. Liberal feminists endorse reproductive freedom for all women. So it also fights for the eradication of the social, political, economic, and legal obstacles that refuse women the same freedom as men. Others liberal feminists criticize that family reproduces gender and argue that freedom is not possible for women until families are dramatically changed.

Vijay Tendulkar makes an effort to reveal the horrible reality while at the same time giving a voice of liberation in the play KML. He uses his weapon to expose the plight of women in the male-dominated society as well as to raise a voice against patriarchal society. It is a dramatic representation of two women. One is the wretched and uneducated wife, and the other is the educated wife, but society treats them equally. Jaisingh, the protagonist of the play, employs both women for his purpose as a device. It is asserted, "Kamala is an indictment of the success-oriented male society in which women find themselves as mere stepping stones for a man" (Rafiq 65).

Tendulkar exposes the modern-day culture, a blind flight of the people in the play. They want to become reputed in an instant at the cost of losing moral values. The present world is success-oriented and man has become overambitious. He runs madly after fame, name, and money. People also worship them who have fame and name, each field of society has become success-oriented.

Gone are the days when Dr. Ambedkar, Mahatma Phule, and Savitri Bai Phule devoted their entire life and delivered self-less service to change the evils scenario of humanity. They are still known for their self -service and gained the place in heart of large humanity. But today man wants name without any fruitful service to humanity. We can find the same picture of a selfish, success-oriented generation of modern India in journalism.

Since long women have been the victims of exploitations. They have been the victims of exploitations in different fields in their life. They are tortured and exploited physically, socially, mentally and economically. There are numerous events of sexual as well as moral exploitations very often drawn attention to by the media. Yet many of those incidents also remain unexplored.

The dark picture of violence against women, sexual harassment, and exploitation of womenis not a new representation; it can be traced in ancient history. Women meet problems in every sphere of life in India. Although the country is fast developing, discrimination on the basis of sex seems to continue. There are various stages of discrimination against women. The decreasing sex-ratio reveals discrimination shown towards women at the very stage of birth. Moreover, women are victims of such crimes as rape, kidnapping, and abduction, dowry-related crimes, molestation, sexual harassment; eve-teasing, etc. The long prevailed male supremacy over female in the patriarchal set-up of the society is greatly responsible for such victimization. The torture in family and society, harassment at workplaces and trafficking for sex are some of the evils still widespread.

Indian woman is assumed to bear the stamp of cultured living through self-sacrifice, physical exertion, and mental endurance. She is regarded as a symbol of compassion. In spite of the fact that India is developing as a global power but in reality, and in practical life, half of its population is far away from the progress of the nation. The women, irrespective of their class, caste and educational status have to struggle to live life with dignity. A woman is simply a woman. But the woman is defined in terms of her relationship to serve patriarchy. Her position as a woman is overtaken by her being as a mother a sister a wife or a daughter.

In the era of growing consumerism and commercialism in otherwise, an objective sector like journalism violence against women has been increasing and a legitimate human right issue in connection to their socio-economic stability has got an impetus.

Vijay Tendulkar was a pioneer of the experimental theatre movement in Marathi as well as a guide of it. He actively involved in civil liberties movements in Maharashtra. This shows his great concern for his country, humanities, and the deprived class of society particular women. Exposing the flaws and the inevitable failure of a human being in his pla Tendulkar exposes modern-day culture, a blind flight of the people in the play. They want to become reputed in an instant at the cost of losing moral values. The present world is success-oriented, and man has become overambitious. He runs madly after fame, name, and money. People also worship them who have fame and names; each field of society has become success-oriented.

Gone are the days when Dr. Ambedkar, Mahatma Phule, and Savitri Bai Phule devoted their entire lives and delivered selfless service to change the evil scenario of humanity. They are still known for their self-service and have gained the place in the hearts of large humanity. But today man wants name without any fruitful service to humanity. We can find the same picture of a selfish, success-oriented generation of modern India in journalism.

Since long, women have been the victims of exploitation. They have been the victims of exploitation in different fields in their lives. They are tortured and exploited physically, socially, mentally, and economically. There are numerous events of sexual as well as moral exploitation very often drawn attention to by the media. Yet many of those incidents also remain unexplored.

The dark picture of violence against women, sexual harassment, and exploitation of women is not a new representation; it can be traced in ancient history. Women meet problems in every sphere of life in India. Although the country is fast developing, discrimination on the basis of sex seems to continue. There are various stages of discrimination against women. The decreasing sex-ratio reveals discrimination shown towards women at the very stage of birth. Moreover, women are victims of such crimes as rape, kidnapping, and abduction, dowry-related crimes, molestation, sexual harassment; eve-teasing, etc. The long-prevailing male supremacy over females in the patriarchal set-up of the society is greatly responsible for such victimization. The torture in family and society, harassment at workplaces, and trafficking for sex are some of the evils still widespread.

Indian women are assumed to bear the stamp of cultured living through self-sacrifice, physical exertion, and mental endurance. She is regarded as a symbol of compassion. In spite of the fact that India is developing as a global power, in reality, and in practical life, half of its population is far away from the progress of the nation. The women, irrespective of their class, caste, and educational status, have to struggle to live life with dignity. A woman is simply a woman. But the woman is defined in terms of her relationship to serve patriarchy. Her position as a woman is overtaken by her being a mother, a sister, a wife, or a daughter. In the era of growing consumerism and commercialism in otherwise objective sectors like journalism, violence against women has been increasing, and a legitimate human rights issue in connection to their socio-economic stability has got an impetus.

Vijay Tendulkar was a pioneer of the experimental theater movement in Marathi as well as a guide of it. He was actively involved in civil liberties movements in Maharashtra. This shows his great concern for his country, the humanities, and the deprived class of society, particularly women. Exposing the flaws and the inevitable failure of a human being in his plays, he becomes a master of the dramatic world. He started writing plays while he worked as a journalist, and that experience reflected frequently in his plays. He becomes a master of dramatic world. He started writing plays while he worked as a journalist and that experience reflect frequently in his plays.

Tendulkar penned *Kamala* is characteristically topical and intensely sentimental. Exploitation and oppression of women are the sorts of Indian society for centuries, and Tendulkar gives a vivid picture of reality in the play. The play demonstrates, more or less, how women are exploited in various ways, how they understand, and how they fight for their identity. The inhuman treatment that they receive from the male-dominated society indicates that they lose their freedom first and their lives later for the sake of men. The playwright deals with the theme of gender deformity in his plays. We also see here that the play also exposes more deeply the voice of women's liberation. By exposing the liberation of women, Tendulkar becomes feminist.

Tendulkar is obsessed with individual rights for liberty. He intends to play the role of a socially aware person and uses the stage to articulate the voice of protest against all types of exploitation. His mission is not to give moral and ethical massage but to project social problems.

The play *Kamala* where we find three levels of exploitation of women in the male-dominated Indian society. The first level is the exploitation of tribal women, Kamala. She is sold in the flesh market like any commodity or thing as if she has no human feelings or aspirations. Jaisingh Jadhav, the journalist buys her, intending to use her as a socio-political instrument to bring into the light the existence of human flesh-market in the country.

The second subjugation is presented in the form of Sarita, Jaisingh's wife. He treats her as his private possession, a puppet, and a compliant servant. Through the character of Sarita, we get to know the status of the woman as a wife in the typical Indian patriarchal system. Sarita discards her identity when she becomes wife Jaisingh. She makes herself busy with domestic activity. Being unaware of her exploitation, she mutely bears a lot of suffering in the house. Kamala is a woman who opens Sarita's eyes and shows a new world of her existence.

The third type of exploitation is revealed in the play as the economic suppression of women. It is seen through the character of the maidservant, Kamalabai. She is often reproached by her master, Jaisingh, who speaks of leaving the house but is unable to leave so. Thus, the feministic perspective on *Kamala* is multi-dimensional. It is sociopolitical, familial, and economical, as represented by the three female characters like Kamala, Sarita, and Kamalabai, respectively. Simone speaks the truth:

> The woman has always been man's dependent, if not his slave; the two sexes have never shared the world inequality. And even today

> woman is heavily handicapped, though her situation is beginning to change. Almost nowhere is her legal status the same as men and frequently it is much to her disadvantage. (20)

Vijay Tendulkar projects all three women on the basis of realism. They are plunged under the pressure of patriarchy. Jaisingh Jadhav exploits all three women and makes the utmost use of their lives to gain position and reputation in the family and society. His policy of 'use and throw' regarding Kamala is the obvious and uppermost peak of his hypocrisy. As mentioned, the sufferers of his hypocrisy are three different women belonging to three different strata of society. Kamala is the lowest in the order, hence is the most oppressed one. Similarly, Kamalabai too belongs to the lower strata, and her poverty makes her helpless.

Sarita, though educated, is also a victim of a male-dominated family and society. As a wife, she is taken for granted and has to follow the orders of her husband. In other words, the play has realistically presented the exploitation of women belonging to any class, atmosphere, or region. It truthfully focuses on the point that women are always at the giving end and are voiceless victims of male dominance. Tendulkar has successfully handled the burning issue of subjugation of women in the family in the play, *Kamala.*

Being an individualist, Tendulkar presents an individual versus society. We can easily perceive his concerns for individual freedom in his plays. It appears that he leaves ethical questions to the discretion of his audience. Asha Kanwar's remark proves his individual intensity: "By leaving ethical questions open, Tendulkar is perhaps inviting his audience to think about the solutions for themselves" (33).

Kamala, published in 1981, was originally written in Marathi and later translated by Priya Adarkar. The play exposes also the hypocritical attitude of society towards women. It draws attention towards issues like the flesh market, the condition of typical Indian women (as portrayed through the characters of Sarita and Kamala), and the unsolved friction in the marital lives of Indian couples, etc.

The prize of Kamala in the flesh market is very low only two hundred and fifty rupees. It may feel imaginative, but the play KML is based on a real-life incident. A correspondent editor with *The Indian Express*, named Ashwin Sarin had brought a girl from rural flesh market and presented her at the press conference. The incident created great uproar and tumult. It also provided stimulate to the imagination of Tendulkar who in KML exercised the same incident to throw the light on the mundane reality of flesh market in the country as well as the position of women in society.

Similarly, we see the hypocritical nature of success-oriented contemporary journalists and find the die-hard competition in journalism. Tendulkar criticizes the flaws of the so-called sophisticated, modern, and success-oriented society where the people are seen following their material goals while neglecting human emotions and values. As a result, Jaisingh, who is too obsessed with success, breaks down mentally at the end as he is also dismissed from his post.

The issue of newspaper reporting is presented in a very critical manner in the play. The so-called medium of social reform, the newspaper, degenerates into an object of fame and material success. The reporters can go to any extent, like using the pathetic condition of the woman like Kamala and presenting her at the press conference as a steep stone. The so-called sophisticated and success-oriented journalist is represented through the character of Jaisingh Jadhav, who leaves Kamala to her own fate as soon as his purpose is fulfilled.

The questions asked to Kamala at the press conference are indicative that they throw a flashlight on how society is interested in the victimization of a woman or helpless beings. Kamala is ruthlessly exposed and presented in her tattered clothes, but none of the members present come forward to rescue her. It confirms that patriarchy still exists and humiliates women in many respects.

The play also attempts a serious critique of the family system in India. In the traditional family system, women are mere slaves, servants, as against their male companions. Sarita recognizes her real status in the house at the end of the play. She becomes conscious of her husband's double standard and hypocritical nature and feels like a puppet in the hands of Jaisingh. For him, there is no difference between Sarita's position and that of Kamala's.

All the three female characters are dominated and tyrannized by Jaisingh Jadhav, the master in *Kamala*. He creates his complete power and controls them. As we see, patriarchy comes to his aid in this respect. He is a typical representative of the Indian male dominating society. His wife, Sarita, servant, Kamalabai, and the woman bought, Kamala, are all easy prey for him as they have also come from the same society and accepted their fate as subordinates to the male-masters.

Outwardly, the playwright depicts the institution of marriage through husband-wife relationship but inwardly he criticizes it. The wife, Sarita works almost like a slave for her husband Jaisingh, in spite of educated and from an aristocratic family. Her condition is not different from that of the woman like Kamala. She passively and unknowingly accepts this condition. In the social ladder, the positions of both women differ greatly. It is Kamala; the woman at the lower end of social structure makes Sarita realize her subordinate and trivial position in the house. This picture of grim reality shows patriarchal culture.

In a nutshell, the play throws flashlight on the truth of the modern world. It clearly provides a vivid picture of social obligations, the ruthlessness of media, a true picture of journalism, a racket of flesh market, the condition of helpless oppressed women, a phenomenon of dominance and bondage. The play is an exposition of male chauvinism that rarely provides women's liberation. The life story of Kamala and Sarita is proof of the fact that women cannot think out of the gender-determined structure.

The two-act play, KML begins and as we find that the central action takes places in a fashionable drawing room. Telephonic talks as the major backdrop of dramatic action. The audience sees that Sarita attending calls at the same time working in the kitchen and speaking on the phone. The dialogues that follow, the phone call discloses that Sarita has to note down all incoming calls. Kakasaheb, her uncle hails from Phaltan village; he also runs a newspaper in vernacular language. Kakasaheb is irritated by looking at this mechanical exercise of Sarita. She has no choice to assert in the house. Sarita accepts and expresses," That's the way you see it, my husband, differently. If I say they didn't tell me their name he gets angry with me for not asking" (Act 1.3). Engage in household activities, the repeated phone calls and the involuntary response of Sarita confirms that she is a perfect Indian wife of Jaising Jadhav.

Jaising Jadhav never tells her wife whereabouts whenever he is out of the house. Meanwhile, she gets the information on Jadhav's arrival. She hurriedly cleans the house before Jaisingh's arrival, takes care of satisfying his physical needs and providing domestic comfort. She immediately orders for vegetables, sweets, and beer in advance. Even she neglects the departure of her uncle. She is so busy with household activities. Kakasaheb, seeing her home-centered approach, says, "You may be highly educated, Sarita, but you are still a girl from the old Mohitwada!" (Act 1. 5).

Thus, in all her actions and behavior, she executes the role of a typical representative wife who is a mere slave to her master or male partner. Feminist, John Stuart Mill believes in individual freedom. As a champion of individual freedom, Mill, in his famous work *The Subjection of Women* (1869), expresses disapproval of the system as 'domestic slavery' and identifies the need for educational and economic strength for the women.

Jaisingh Jadhav's arrival with Kamala, a village woman, is the main action in the play. She appears in her rage with a bundle in the corner of her arm. As if a commodity, she has been brought by him for some two hundred and fifty rupees from Bihar. Kamala is about to present at the press conference in order to highlight the existence of the flesh trade in the remote parts of villages in India. Kamala, on the other hand, is ignorant of happenings, thinks that she has been brought there to enact as the mistress of Jadhav. When Kamala comes, Sarita has not the courage to ask her husband and passively allows her husband. The event suggests that a married woman cannot think out of the house.

Kakasaheb informs Jadhav about threatening phone calls, but Jadhav does not seem surprised, rather, he laughs as it was a routine for him. Kakasaheb wants to know the purpose of Jaisingh regarding the position of Kamala. He is surprised by knowing the selfish intention. Kakaaheb was also a journalist, but he never thought of using the power of journalism for his personal name and fame. Kakasaheb confesses, "I am a back number –a remnant of times past. A dead journalist who's just about staying alive now is the day of your husband's type of journalism. The high –speed type" (Act 1. 5).

In modern journalism, the press is no longer a voice of people, but it is a method to monopolize the resources of power for its own benefit. There is no value in people› emotions and sentiments. Like an Indian wife, Sarita tries to defend her husband by presenting the modern-day picture of news related to rape, bloodshed; murder, and atrocity before Kakasaheb. For Kakasaheb, the press was an instrument to inspire the spirit of nationalism, while for Jaisingh, it is a means to achieve personal success. He uses the press as a powerful instrument to impose his authority on the powerless. He also admits, "Not on the people, on bad trends. I have no objection, no concern with individuals "(Act 1.11). It strikes us with the harsh reality of journalism and the intention of Jasinigh.

He shows his power of journalism when argues, "I needed evidence, didn't I? Do you. I turned the world upside down to find this bazaar. I was the first journalist to reach it. Today I'm going to throw the whole caboodle in the governments 'lap – along with the evidence. Just watch!" (Act 1.15). He warns and challenges on the base of his evidence. It shows his anger and ego.

Sarita is seen behaving like a typical product of the patriarchal system that always supports her husband. She regards it as a sacred duty to please her husband and shares her joys as well as sorrows of her husband. She sometimes becomes the object of uncle's criticism and even the friend of Jaisingh, Jain taunts her as "lovely bonded laborer" (Act 1.17). She sometimes feels irritated by Jaisingh's over-enthusiasm and dominant nature. But it is obvious that she has accepted him whole-heartedly as a dutiful wife. She accepts his virtues as well as follies. As a typical, doting wife she has no grudge to accept her identity as the wife of a reputed newspaper journalist and regards her function is to serve the interests of her husband. Commenting on the plot construction of the play, N.S. Dharan speaks out:

> *Kamala* is a two-act play, designed on the mode of the popular dramatic construct of the present century. There are no scene

> divisions of the acts. The plots are expertly structured so that, the denouement unravels itself as "reversal". The phone calls also serve to indicate how slavish and claustrophobic atmosphere. (62)

The second act opens, and the audience sees Jadhav in a jubilant mood celebrating with his friend Jain. Neglecting Kakasaheb and his wife, he celebrates his temporary'success 'at the press conference. Jadhav and Jain drink and revel and regard the event at a press conference as 'fun'. Sarita and Kakasaheb are irritated by their fun and insensitivity. Kakasaheb rebukes Jadhav, and the later gets angry. When Jain and Kakasaheb leave, Jadhav wants to go bedroom at once with Sarita, but she refuses his amorous advances. Jadhav gets dejected and begins to abuse her.

On learning that Sarita bore no children, Kamala sympathizes with her and offers that she will produce children for her and the family. Sarita is amazed at Kamala's simplicity, at the same time, the conversation with Kamala opens her eyes. She realizes that, though educated, she too functions as a mere pawn in the hands of her husband and that she is nothing more than the object to satisfy his carnal desires.

Jaisingh Jadhav is an ambitious and adventurous journalist. He would work very devotedly for his employer, Seth Singhania, the owner of an English newspaper. He is always ready to take risks in order to render the anti-social elements in society. He leaves no stone unturned to bring out the social maladies into the light. Outwardly, Jaisingh appears to be a sincere champion working for a social cause. But in reality, he chases after name, fame, and money. He would tread any path or go to any extent to fulfill his ambition. He shows but very little care for the feelings of his wife Sarita and makes her work almost like a slave. Tendulkar presents the hypocrisy and double standard nature of Jaisingh through the 'Kamala' episode. He buys Kamala from a rural flesh market for Rs. 250, intending to present Kamala in a press conference to prove the existence of the flesh trade in the remote part of the country.

He tells Kakasaheb that presently he is concerned with his successful'mission' of presenting Kamala as a proof of the existence of flesh trade in the nation. Sarita is shocked by Jaisingh's doings and insensitivity regarding the 'exhibition' of a woman. Kamala does not like to be there in the press conference in tattered clothes, but Jadhav insists she remain as she is. Kamala agrees to be with him in her clothes. By now it should be clear that he is overambitious and a handman.

He is so hypocritical that he would not allow Kamala even to bathe or change her tattered clothes as they would serve his purpose, namely, presenting Kamala before the public her miserable and hopeless condition so that he can succeed in gaining an appreciation for rescuing a victim like Kamala. He wants to use Kamala as an instrument for his reputation. Shailaja Wadikar observes, "Jaisingh uses Kamala as a means by which he can get a promotion in his job and win reputation in his professional career" (24). It is obvious that he is not really concerned about the plight of helpless women.

Vijay Tendulkar has radical views on women's liberation. He firmly believes that women themselves ought to be determined to liberate themselves. Nobody can come and liberate them from the suppression and limitations of patriarchy. But here we observe that the wretched condition of Kamala raises new energy and new consciousness in Sarita. By collecting her confidence, she argues:

SARITA.She is a woman, after all. And her sari is torn.

JAISINGH. (His voice rising). I know. I know! You don't have to tell me, understand? I have a very good idea of all that. I want her to look just as she is at the Press Conference. It's very important.

SARITA.All right. (Exist) (Act 1. 22)

It proves that Sarita forewarns her husband for her liberation. Vijay Tendulkar represents the voice of the subaltern woman who mutely bears the suffering. They are weak and helpless. Despite her resistance, Sarita fails to raise her voice against her husband because she is a wife and expected not to be raised voice against the husband.

Through the titular character of his play *Kamala*, Tendulkar has shed light on the miserable condition of ignorant and helpless women in our exploitative and male-dominated society. Kamala is exploited by Jaisingh, the male protagonist of the play, for the fulfillment of his journalistic ambition. Kamala is an ignorant and poor tribal woman and is so ignorant to perceive what exactly her buyer's intentions are. She simply thinks that Jaisingh has brought her to keep her as his mistress. She submits to her lot and does not care to which place her 'owner' may take her. When Jaisingh brings her to his house he asks her:

JAISINGH. How do you like here, Kamala?

KAMALA.Very much, Sahib.

JAISINGH. Kamala, this evening we're going out together.

KAMALA.Oh! I'll see Bombay! They say it's a very big city. (Act 1.19)

She does not know whether she is in Delhi or in Bombay. Jaisingh takes advantage of her innocent and ignorant nature. He lies to her that there will be 'big feasts' for you and the people would like to meet her at the press conference. Kamala feels pleased, but she does not like to go there in her tattered clothes as she is going to see the 'big city' and its people. In all her gestures, she reveals her kindness and rural simplicity. But the career-oriented journalist, Jadhav, wants to create 'great uproar' in journalism by exhibiting the victimization of women at certain places. He commands Kamala to remain in her rags, and the victim, Kamala, has to obey the orders of her'master'

She has no objection to it because she has no alternative but to follow the order of the master. She accepts Jaisingh as her master wholeheartedly and is ready to do anything for him. She probably feels that it is the destiny of women like her. She imagines that Jaisingh is going to keep her as his mistress. Kamala has not only been the victim of her circumstance, but the man like Jaisingh, with his'social purpose' too, exploits her and treats her as inhuman.

The play shows an ideal image of a woman in the first act. Jaisingh highlights the corrupt practices that prevailed in the society. He criticizes others, but at the same time, he does not hesitate to practice them in his own life. Here we find the distinction of reality and illusion in the confession Jaisingh:

> Someone has got to hold back the uncontrolled license of those who have the machinery of power in their hands. The weak and backward

> sections of society are under attack need someone to make a noise against it. The common man is living in a-a king of unconscious haze today. He needs to be shocked into liking at the truth now and then. We need a force that will raise his consciousness, prepare him to struggle for social and political change. (Act 1.24)

In the first act two women Sarita and Kamala remain marginalized and appear only as of the others. Sarita is marginalized in two ways. First, she is a woman and second, she is a wife. Similarly, Kamala is also marginalized by three respects. First, she is a woman, second is poor and illiterate and third she is picked up from the flesh market. Kamalabai is marginalized by one way that she is totally dependent on Jaisingh's house.

Kamala's simplicity sees when she thinks the reality of her life is applicable to all women in general. The interchange of the personal emotion of Sarita and Kamala suggests that woman have great underrating of their fellow woman. She thinks that the women like Kamalabai and Sarita too must have been purchased by Jaisingh. She asks Sarita:

> KAMALA. Can I ask you something? You won't be angry?
>
> SARITA. No, go on.
>
> KAMALA. How much did he buy you for? (Act 2.34)

When Kamala is tired and, in her sleep, Jaisingh would not let her sleep peacefully. He is concerned only with his own success. He asks Sarita:

> JAISINGH. What's she doing?
>
> SARITA. She is asleep. She isn't feeling well.
>
> JAISINGH. Wake her up.
>
> SARITA. She's only just gone off to sleep
>
> JAISINGH. Never mind. Wake her up and send her here. I want to talk to her. (Act 2.18-19)

The pain of being a childless woman is a serious issue in Indian society. The condition of such a woman becomes miserable. The people in a society mostly attribute the barrenness to the woman, whereas the man is considered flawless. Vijay Tendulkar frequently shows the problem of a childless woman. The issue also finds in SKB, where Laxmi is thrown away by her husband because she is unable to birth a baby. Society criticizes such a woman. Being a rural and tribal woman, Kamala could perceive the problem of Sarita, though practically there is no problem on the issue of children in Sarita's house. She is ready to bear children for her; "I'll have as many as you want" (Act 2.34). It reveals that Kamala wants to stay permanently in Jasingh's house and changes her. Though she is illiterate and naive, she has full of sympathy for the childless woman like Sarita. She expresses that she would make the house a worthwhile and pleasant place to live in. She has her offer for Sarita:

> Memsahib, if you won't misunderstand, I'll tell you. The master bought you, he bought me too. So, memsahib, both of us may stay here like sisters. We will keep the master happy. The master will have children. I'll do the hard work, and I'll bring forth the children. I'll bring them up. You keep the accounts and run the house...Fifteen days of the month, you sleep with the master, the other fifteen, I'll sleep with him. Agreed? (Act 2.35)

After noticing that Jaisingh has no children from Sarita, she is ready to take that responsibility upon herself. She asks Sarita to look after the work of giving company to Jaisingh in society, whereas she will take care of producing an heir for him. This acceptance of Kamala proves that women know their role of childbearing. This responsibility hinders women from liberation and retains them in the four walls.

The names of Kamalabai, a maidservant, and Kamala resemble very much. Kamalabai too works very hard for a meager salary. She expresses her desire for returning to her native place in front of Sarita. She does not care for Kamala and her misfortunes; on the contrary, she hates her and scolds her in the fear of losing her job. She is also dominated by her master, Jadhav, and treated like a slave. Often, she shows her displeasure and utters to leave the house, but is unable to do so. Her character suggests the complete surrender of women due to poverty. Kamalabai expresses her anger when Sarita offers her Sari to Kamala. She speaks, "Your sari – for her? (Act 2. 38). In spite of being a woman, Kamalabai's attitude towards Kamala suggests that she does not feel any sympathy for Kamalabai's wretched condition and looks down upon her. It is an example of a woman's insensitivity towards other women.

The press conference was outwardly held to expose the existence of flesh trade in the country and the sexual harassment of a helpless woman like Kamala. But in reality, she is harassed physically and psychologically and oppressed at the press conference. She has to undergo unpleasant queries as:

> If there is free sex among you, what do you do with illegitimate children? .... How many men have you slept with? (Act 2.29)

Kamala sits silent feeling embarrassed but can't do anything against her victimization while Jaisingh and Jain, the self- proclaimed 'saviours' drink and enjoy.

Kamala's entry into the house reveals the selfish hypocrisy that is practiced by Sarita and the inconsequentiality of her existence. It also opens all every thread of weaving ball of marriage at the same time as the authenticity of modern marriage. Sarita lives in the fantasy realism of her husband. Kamala shakes this revelation and touches her deeply with the soul. She feels helpless and tries to futilely search for the meaning of marriage. Sarita admits:

> I was asleep... Kamala woke me up. With a shock. Kamala showed me everything... I saw that the man I thought the partner was the master of a slave... I have no right at all in the house... slaves don't have rights, do Kakasaheb?...Dance to their master's whim. Laugh, when he says, laugh. Cry, when he says, cry. When he says to pick the phone, they must pick it up...when he says, lie on the bed- she (She is twisted in pain). (Act 2.46)

At this juncture of the play, Sarita begins to understand her own rights, roles, wishes and all activities in the house. She is distressed to see that in fact there is little difference between Kamala and herself. But at the same time, we find that Kamala is completely aware of her position and therefore accepts that the person (Jaisingh) who has bought her will be her master and he is no less than god for her. She accepts him completely i.e. mentally as well as physically.

She is ready to submit completely to her master-buyer owing to her upbringing in such an atmosphere where buying and selling of girls were fully accepted. In her society, women were considered as a means of making money. The members of society make ascertain that the sold girl should fulfil the wishes of her buyer. She should please the owner-master in every respect. She should please him by doing all the household works, gratifying his physical needs, producing children and looking after them. She may not be his wedded wife or may be called a keep, but she should perform the duties of a wife.

Moreover, women like Kamala internalize that they have to sacrifice and lead life according to the desires of their master. Such women are treated almost like animals or even worse. Their status is that of a slave or bonded labourer. Kamala is thus representative of her class. She is an embodiment of total surrender to male-dominance. In all her simplicity she is even pleased to join the household and ready to do everything for her master who ultimately sends her to the orphanage once his aim is fulfilled.

Through the character of Sarita, Tendulkar has depicted a truthful picture of a modern Indian woman who is trapped between the opposite trails of tradition and modernity. According to Shibu Simon, "Tendulkar exposes the chauvinism intrinsic in the modern Indian male who believes himself to be liberal through his delineation of Sarita's character" (187). Her ambitious husband treats her like a doll or puppet in his hands.She gets but very little attention and respect by Jaisingh.

In the case of Sarita who is unaware of subjugation under the guise of duty and responsibility of a wife. Sarita, therefore, revolts against her suppression. On the other hand, Kamala accepts her servility willingly finds her emancipation in the form Jaisingh. She gets liberty from flesh market where is oppressed. Comparatively, she likes to live permanently in this house. She appreciates, "My word! What a big house! [Pause] And so beautiful. Even our raja's house isn't as beautiful" (Act 1. 33). Moreover, she has internalized the norms of patriarchy and identifies her femininity with her servility accordingly.

Though Sarita is an educated urban lady, she seems to be unaware of her own slave-like existence. "The character of Sarita suggests that even a modern, educated woman is not so free as her male counterpart in contemporary society, as she has to follow her husband's whims and caprices in and outside the household life" (Wadikar 84). Jaisingh's attitude towards his wife is not much different from that of Kamala. Sarita is treated as an object of enjoyment and as a slave to look after the house.

While Jaisingh goes out from home for long periods, she looks after everything submissively. She does everything that is possible to make him happy. She notes down the name of every caller asking for Jaisingh. She is conscious that failure on her part will cause displeasure to her husband. Her husband, on the other hand, takes the least care to tell her anything about his outing, as Sarita says, "He is gone out somewhere" (Act 1.6). The phone calls form a recurrent motif in the play and contribute to the main theme of the play. They serve to indicate Jadhav's preoccupation and how busy the journalist he is.

Those phone calls also hint at the slavish following of Jaisingh's orders by Sarita. When she receives the message that Jaisingh is returning from the newspaper office, in her all hustle and bustle, she makes arrangements for his reception. She, in all her gestures and concerns at the beginning of the play, reveals her sensitiveness to her husband's needs, requirements, pleasures, likes, and dislikes, etc. Observing Sarita's alacrity, Kakasaheb, her uncle, wonders how an educated girl like Sarita could behave like a slave to her husband. He frankly tells her that she may be "highly educated, but still a girl from old Mohite Wada" (Act 1. 5). The irony is that the self-absorbed journalist, Jaisingh, does not give any importance to the fact that Sarita's support and encouragement have helped him in building a successful career.

When Jaisingh brings Kamala in the house, Sarita is shocked to hear that he has bought her for two hundred and fifty rupees from Bihar. She is surprised when Jaisingh tells her, "they sell human beings at this bazaar. They have an open auction for women of all sorts of ages" (Act 1.14). She feels embarrassed at the further description of the bazaar and asks Jaisingh to stop, for, she does not like the very idea of an exhibition of a woman. Jaisingh warns her not to reveal it to anyone until the 'event' of the press conference. Out of her sympathy and humanity, she would give a bath and fresh sari to Kamala but Jaisingh rejects the very idea indifferently.

Sarita gets disgusted at the narration of happenings by Jaisingh and Jain at the press conference. She questions them rather surprisingly that "while they were asking her those terrible questions, and making fun of her- you just sat and watched, did you?" (Act 2. 30). But Jaisingh shows total indifference and sticks to his so-called success. He believes that he has successfully brought the "criminal sale of human beings into the light of the day" (Act 2.31). Jain's remarks throw light on Jaisingh's nature as well as the status of Sarita. He remarks that:

> Hi Bhabhiji, I mean, an English 'hi' to him, and Marathi 'hai'(alas) to you. This warrior against exploitation in the country is exploiting you...Shame on you! Hero of anti-exploitation campaigns makes a slave of wife. (Act 1.17)

The statement hints at Jaisingh's treatment of his wife, which is an open secret known to all and sundry. But Jaisingh wants that Sarita should not discuss her sorrows and grievances with anybody, especially with outsiders. It is contrary action of Jaisingh. On the one side, he exposes the flesh market of women at the Press conference on the other side he cannot stop the exploitation of wife in his house. It confirms the hypocrisy of her husband.

As we know the nature of man, being a social animal, he has to live in society. Man always tries to present himself as something different than others. This distinctiveness composes his individuality, which is an outcome of his self- identity and self- consciousness. Some question like "Who am I?" and "What am I?" assists a man to recognize his own identity.

Socio-economic, political, religious and cultural aspects affect the process of self- identity. Many people fail to understand their own true self particularly women. Because every society has different social structures which form some values, customs, and traditions. It laid down some rules, that society accepts unknowingly them as its own. This kind of structure and acceptance is the main barrier in the realization of 'Self'

The same conflict takes place among all women in general and Indian women in particular. Right from the beginning, they have not only been treated as inferior, emotional, physically weak, biologically and economically different, and something 'else, but they have also conditioned their minds. They are simply used as an object of sexual gratification and considered unfit for independence.

The goal of our lives is to know ourselves, and people constantly strive for, but rarely reach it. After a long time and continuous struggle, women got success in gaining their rights. Education enlightened their lives and gave them new insights, but the fact is that the success of an individual is not only determined by her academic achievement but primarily by self-awareness, self-consciousness, and self-knowledge that still lack in women's lives.

Kamala's arrival is the turning point in Sarita's life. Sarita might not have been aware of her exploitation if Kamala had not come into contact with Sarita. After realizing her position in the house, she begins to define her identity and raise a voice of emancipation. When she sees Jaisingh using Kamala, whom he has bought to prove the prevalence of flesh-trade, as a commodity, her legs shiver, and her eyes are opened. She gets to know Jaisingh's real attitude of looking at her as only an object of enjoyment and as a caretaker of the house. Shailaja Wadikar observes that "Sarita realizes that she is bound to her husband in the wedlock to slave for him permanently after the entry of Kamala in her house" (77).

We can see a drastic change in her behavior. Sarita determines to change her condition and starts asserting her individuality. There is a marked change in her behavior towards her husband. Earlier, she used to defend Jaisingh in whatever he did. Now she starts defying him. When Jain leaves the house, Jaisingh wants to go to the bedroom with Sarita. She refuses to submit to Jaisingh's desire for physical intimacy. JAISINGH. Come upstairs

SARITA. (Emphatically, without even realizing it) No.

JAISINGH. I'll have my dinner afterward. We'll both eat together.

SARITA.(Without losing her self-control.) Uh-hunh, let me go, I've got work to do.

JAISINGH.(Trying to embrace her). Work later. Come upstairs now.

SARITA.(Throwing him aside with a single shove). Move aside. What are you doing?

JAISINGH. (Hurt), what's the matter? What did I do? Why are you making a face like that? Why did you push me away? You've never done that before. (Act 2.32).

But when Sarita denies his advances the representative of Patriarchal-husbands, Jaisingh gets furious and asks Sarita "Don't I have the right to have my wife when I feel like it? Don't I? I'm hungry for that too- I've been hungry for six days. Is it a crime to ask for it? Answer me!" (Act 2.32).Catherine Thankamma'sremark is very contextual to understand the nature of her husband, "Jaisingh remains totally indifferent to Sarita's feelings. He expects Sarita to submit to his desire for intercourse whether she wants it or not and calls her a 'bitch' when she refuses to cooperate with him" (81).

Sarita resists to his decision of sending Kamala to the orphanage. From docile woman, she transforms herself defiant and assertive. Her power of defense indicates that she wants to create her own world without any assistance from her husband.

SARITA.(With greater determination). Kamala is not going to come with you.

JAISINGH. That is enough of your jokes. Chalo Kamala. (To Sarita) Bring her bundle from inside.

SARITA. Kamala is not goingwith you. She's going to stay here. (Act 2.41)

Above all, Jaisingh is husband so he is more powerful than Sarita. The conflict raises here because Sarita is weak and powerless. An egoistic husband, scolds her with the following words suggests suppression of both women:

It's I who takes decisions in this house, and no one else. Do you understand? I'll be back tonight – if there are any phone calls, say I've gone straight to the office, and write them down…I can't keep Kamala at home. Or we will lose the case against me for buying

> Kamala. I could even be sent to jail. That's why Kamala has to stay in the orphanage... (Act 2.42)

These words certainly disheartened Sarita. This is the moment when Sarita realizes the truth: she is just like Kamala, an obedient servant to her husband. She is a symbol of slavery in the family system. She is perfectly trapped and confined by the bonds of the patriarchy, which marginalizes her. In this way, both Kamala and Sarita are only puppets in the hands of Jaisingh, pleasing their master without any power in their hands.

The total control is concentrated in the hands of the head of a family, that is, Jaisingh, who enjoys his power without any resistance. By now she realizes fully that her husband is self-centered and opportunistic and has lost humanity. He has so fallen from a life that he has used Kamala as an instrument to gain reputation, fame, and promotion. He is not loyal to his profession, and he has even violated the principles of his job, journalism. He is concerned only about getting success; his unfaithfulness and selfishness make her decide to leave him. Even at the cost of others. Due to his unfaithfulness and selfishness, she decides to leave him.

After leaving Kamala to "Nari Niketan', Jadhav asks Sarita to accompany him to a party. But Sarita stoutly rejects his proposal. At this juncture of the play, we find Sarita is a changed woman who would even convene a press conference to expose the real nature of her husband. Her uncle gets surprised to notice the change in her relationship with her husband. She is so angry and frustrated because of her husband's behavior that she thinks of arranging a press conference to expose Jaisingh in front of the world.

> I am going to present a man who in the year 1982 still keeps a slave, right here in Delhi. Jaisingh Jadhav. I am going to say this man's a great advocate of freedom. And he brings home a slave and exploits her... Listen to the story of how he bought the slave Kamala and made use of her. The other slave he got free—not just free—the slave's father shelled out the money--- a big sum. (Act 2.46)

Kakasaheb seems startled, asks Sarita what exactly has happened between them. She simply replies that it is "marriage" (Act 2.41).We know that marriage signifies a transfer of the woman from her natal group to her husband's group in patriarchy. In the real world, many problems of women are associated with marriage, like customs of dowry, age of marriage, bride's wealth, divorce and separation, widowhood, and remarriage. Marriage is also the accessible path of women's oppression. A woman forgets her own world when she enters the world of her husband. Another aspect of marriage is the humiliation and oppression of women in the four walls. Here we witness Sarita also becoming a victim of the institution of marriage. However, it is also seen that women are far away from economic responsibility, and they live a carefree life.

The well-knit plot-construction of the play compassionates to think about the word "Marriage" as Sarita answers Kakasaheb about the change in her. Dr. Ravi Chopra observes:

> Marriage provides the opportunity to enable commonality of thought and feeling between the two. Wife and Husband lived together for developing love which is not merely flame melting flame but spirit calling to spirit. Marriage was not an end in itself but the means of gaining self- fulfillment. Man and woman must realize their complementariness and base their relationship on equality and mutual respect. (36)

In our country, marriage has been regarded as a pure and sanctified institution. But due to deprivation and degradation in such sacred institutions at present times, one is compelled to feel that this institution, in fact, serves to provide a slave in the form of a wife to their male masters in our society. Thus, the play exposes this kind of situation. The social hypocrisy and its duality offer no protection to women and instead turn them into slaves.

The life of Indian married women is totally based on various types of obligations. The play raises certain fundamental questions regarding the value system of a modern man who is ready to sacrifice human values in the name of humanity itself. Vijay Tendulkar, as stated elsewhere, only highlights the condition of a married woman but doesn't give any suggestions or solutions. His treatment of the subject and his concerns with feminism are indirect and covert. Linda Hutcheon's opinion is important in the context of the present discussion. Sheo pines that:

> While feminism and postmodernism have both worked to help us understand the dominant modes of representation at work in our society, feminists have focused on the specifically female subject of representations and have begun to suggest ways of challenging and changing those dominants in both mass culture and high art. They have taught us that to accept unquestioningly any fixed representation --in fiction, film, advertising or whatever --is to condone social systems of power which validate and authorized some images of women (or blacks, Asians, gays, etc.) and others. Cultural production is carried on within a social context and an ideology and lived value system --and it is to this that feminist work has made us pay attention. (78)

The above assertion of Linda Hutcheon reveals the brutal and bitter facts of Indian society in modern times. Hereby representing the burning issue, Tendulkar tries to capture the attention of readers and audiences. It also proves his inclination towards feminism. Simultaneously, it vividly clarifies that equality and fraternity come as usual but not in practical life. Everyone wants women to behave like dolls. Tendulkar presents the bitter truth of male personality. He shows the stereotype of women through the relationship between Jaisingh and Sarita and provokes the reader to think on the relationship of wife and husband and their shared responsibility towards each other. In his unique way, he touches the psychological insight of human beings.

Sarita finds that she is incapable of making any sacrifices to establish her identity, but soon after the entry of Kamala into the house, she investigates the meaning of her role in the life of Jadhav Jaisingh. She is a literal and sophisticated woman, but she too shares the same fate. She has been the victim of a chauvinistic male oppressor. "Like Kamala, Sarita is also an object in Jadhav's life, an object that provides physical enjoyment, social companionship, and domestic comfort" (Banerjee, xvii). The statement reveals the fact that many women in Indian society sacrifices their being, identity, etc for the sake of their husbands and unfortunately their husband remain indifferent and do not respect their wives. Sarita understands this fact of our male-dominated where female-voice is always undermined Sarah Grimke aptly says:

> Man has subjugated women to his will, used her as a means to promote his selfish gratification, to minister to his sensual pleasure, to be an instrument in promoting his comfort; but never has he desired to elevate her to that rank she was created to fill. He has done all he could do to debase and enslave her mind. (10)

She has become conscious of her identity in the course of life and is determined to change her life in the future. On the contrary, being an independent woman, Leela Benare already knows her to identify still she has to endure a lot in mock-trial in the play *Silence! The Court is in Session.* Tendulkar has portrayed Saritaand Benare as modern women who can explore their inner mind, desires, and ambitions. He has presented them as an image of liberty

Sarita gets a realization of her condition in the house that reminds us of a great feminist Shashi Deshpande. Her character Jaya the protagonist in the novel *That Long silence* also becomes conscious that she has lost self-dignity in the name of marriage. Kamala plays a vital role in Sarita's life so far, the awaking voice against oppression and injustice of her husband. Like many feminists, Tendulkar establishes that the humanity of women can't be suppressed for a long time but it cannot be ignored eternally.

As the principal action of *Silence! The Court is in Session* revolves around Benare, here in *Kamala*; the action revolves round Sarita, the woman protagonist. The action of the *Sakharam Binder* may have a difference in respect of the plays mentioned, still, it is largely concerned with the change of fate in womanizer Sakahram and how he surrenders and become helpless in the end. There is no doubt that Tendulkar reveals his feminine leanings and even feministic ideology through his plays. His plays projects women in direct encounter with their male counterparts. N.S. Dharan regards *Kamala* and *Silence! The Court is in Session* as gyno-centric plays. In his book *The Plays of Vijay Tendulkar* writes that:

> Tendulkar has deliberately given his women characters a greater variety and depth- and thus a definite edge, over to – their male

> counterparts. Benare's emotional outburst at the end of *Silence!* And Sarita's confident and assertive utterances towards the close of Kamala show that both the plays are, beyond question, gyno-centric. (49)

Kamala innocently interrogates, "How much did he buy you for?" (Act2.34). Sarita also replies for seven hindered. This question reveals the reality of Savita's life. Kamala plans her future in the company of Sarita. She wants to be a co-partner and share the family responsibility collectively in the family of Sarita. Even she is ready to share sexual life with Jaisingh. Here Kamala' suggestion is a mockery of the entire patriarchal social structure. The one single suggestion of Kamala ignites Sarita to a reassessment of her position in the family of Jaisingh. The oppression of Kamala transforms into a new current of life that is beyond all traditions and the restrictions. Omvedt asserts:

> Feminist studies aim to present a vital and living portrait of Indian womanhood which supplants the mythic and idealized 'Indian womanhood' of the nationalists or objectified woman of Orthodox anthropology. (4)

There seems to be an obvious difference in the position of Kamala and Sarita, but it is their place that only differs. The basic thread that is the exploitation of women is common among them. Sarita, though educated, is exploited within the four walls of the house and Kamala outside the walls. Jaisingh shows utter indifference to both the women. His wife is a source of inspiration for him throughout his career as a journalist; still, she is neglected by him. Being a detached observer, Tendulkar seems not to take any side. But the audience and the reader could easily perceive his leanings toward Kamala and Sarita. In an interview with Satya Saran and Vimal Patil, Tendulkar opines that:

> When I show is the struggle of a woman; it is not one woman's fight. The individual must have name and identity and caste and background to be credible, but she is not just a woman on the stage, in a particular play. I am writing about her situation, showing that the possibility of a struggle against it exists... By not giving a solution, I leave possibilities open, for whatever course the change may take. When the members of my audience go home and chew on the

> situation, they might be able to see their daughter or sister in the woman's position and come up with a way of changing the situation for her advantage. (37)

But Sarita's consciousness lasts for short duration only, for, she provides emotional support when she comes to know that her husband is sacked from the job. Sarita likes Benare in *STCIS* is representative of modern, educated and sophisticated woman in the society. Still, it is quite obvious that formal education has not uplifted their position. They have to undergo the traditional obstacles of discrimination on the basis of their sex.

Sarita's rebellion, however, is short-lived. She comes to know that Jaisingh has been sacked by his employer. Seeing that Jaisingh is feeling disgruntled at the way he has been treated by his employer, Sarita postpones her rebellion. She is mentally prepared for the struggle with society to assert her self-identity. She tells Kakasaheb that presently she will keep everything in her mind as the situation demands, but she will no longer be a slave to her husband in the future. But she is also, in the words of Shanta Gokhale, "a compassionate human being who defers her rebellion against her husband as he is in an acute need of her moral support" (42).

She forgives him and again removes his shoes, suggesting the same fate of her subordination. Still at the end, considering determination on her face and a calm, steady gaze towards the future, we have a hope that she would leave him and lead her free life.

The dramatic effect is very carefully planned and executed by Tendulkar. The denouement comes at the end of the play. In the final part of the play, dismissal of Jaisingh from his job is probably most surprising to the audience as well as readers. Jaisingh who victimizes Kamala as well as Sarita and he also falls a victim. Tendulkar sheds light on the male egoism, domination, selfishness, and hypocrisy of the modern success-oriented generation through his character.

On the contrary, Sarita and Kamala exhibit simplicity, innocence, generosity, and a spirit of devotion. The objection is being raised to Sarita's sympathy towards Jaisingh by some critics as she provides emotional support and saves him from mental collapse at the end of the play. The environment in which she arrives at the conclusion of leaving her husband and her sympathy seem contradictory to many critics. "However, it appears that Sarita comes to this conclusion not because she lacks any spirit of rebellion but because her husband badly needs her emotional support. The humanitarian ideology is clearly perceptible here in her behavior" (Wadikar 42). By providing him emotional support, Sarita proves her humanitarian attitude towards her husband as well as exposes the universal and natural qualities of a woman. She is definitely a changed personality at the end of the play, as she tells Kakasaheb that:

> I'll go on feeling it. But at present, I am going to lock all that up in a corner of my mind and forget about it...But a day will come ...I will do what I wish, and no one will rule over me. That day has to come. And I'll pay, whatever price I have to pay for it (Her gaze is calm, steadily looking ahead at the future. Determination on her face (Act 2.52)

The words put in the bracket indicate her liberation in the near future. Tendulkar throughthese words not just convey Sarita's determination but reveals his own stance. The question raises here why Sarita shows humanitarian attitude towards her husband and why Jaising treats his wife, Sarita, and Kamala as a stepping stone? The reason may be simple that women possess nature while men deal with culture.

This play is constructed against domestic background especially based on husband-wife relationships. The entire action is executed in the household atmosphere. The play reveals the moral, ethical and social significance of life. The action of most of the plays of Tendulkar's plays revolves around the helpless, dependent and oppressed women. His characters like Benare, Sarita and Jyoti occupy the space of the audience's mind. His plays have no lesson but follow the tradition of woman's liberalization. They advocate equality between sexes. This is evident in the speech of Sarita:

> Why? Why can't men limp behind? Why aren't women ever be masters? Why can't a woman at least ask to live her life the same way as a man? Why must only a man have the right to be a man? Does he have one extra sense? A woman can do everything a man can? (Act 2.47)

It is here that Sarita becomes the mouthpiece of the playwright and questions the authority of man as a man. Jaisingh is shown shorn of his usual arrogance, self-confidence and a pitiable figure at the end of the play. He receives what he has sown. His hypocrisy and selfishness pay him in return. Though Sarita is voiceless, her determination and resolution show strong protest against her husband. Subduing her resentment, Sarita moves to support Jaisingh at last. It is not the sign of her weakness but it is her affirmation of those values in life that ever have been dreams of Indian thinkers.

In the decades during which the Women's Liberation Movement flourished, liberationists successfully changed how women were perceived in their cultures, redefined the socio-economic and the political roles of women in society, and transformed mainstream society.

The existence of the social construction of gender is the principal political problem. Formal and informal sex-based discrimination is also another reason for women's suppression. Towards achieving the equality of women, it is required to eradicate the validity of patriarchy and gender –discrimination structure of society.

So, the overall scanning of the play deduces that the play looks at the burning issue of 'auction of women 'that disturbs a sensitive mind, issues that need to be answered by each of us. The Indian Constitution banned slavery in our country, but unfortunately, it still exists. In the marriage market, it is legalized, and women are sold on the name of tradition. The Dowry system still exists, and selling and buying of humans are common in the tradition and customs.

Vijay Tendulkar represents the aspect of women's liberation in the plays KAM and STCIS. It also shows a compressive thesis on the well-interlinked mechanism of oppression and exploitation. The concept of liberty is linked to power. Kamalabai, the maid, is the slave of Sarita because she is poor and totally dependent on Jaisingh's family for her bread and butter. Kamala becomes a slave because she has been exploited as the object of a flesh market. But she gets consciousness with the reformative zeal of Jaisingh. Sarita depends on her husband because she is the wife of Jaisingh. He also becomes a victim of the circumstances, and she becomes a victim of patriarchal society. Tendulkar brings out the ugliness of women's suppression into the limelight, but their suffering shows others a torch of women's liberation.

The play reveals that the playwright has an inner desire to strive tirelessly for the perfection of life where there are no barriers to caste-class sex or race in society. He dreams and expects a world of harmony rather than disharmony. Like Chekhov, he wants to create a kind, integrated, emotionally refined, and mindful world. The final analysis proves that the playwright wants to liberate us from our cribbed, cabined, and confined existence and helps us to create the one world that is a human world where there is no exploitation of women, no crisis, no conflicts, no violence, and no suffocation of natural desires, only calm and peace.

Works Cited

Chopra, Dr. Ravi. *Advanced Essays.* New Delhi: Bookhive, 1980.Print.

Dharan, N.S. *The Plays of Vijay Tendulkar.* New Delhi: Creative Books, 1999. Print.

Durant, Will. *The Story of Philosophy.* New York: Pocket books, 2006. Print.

Gokhale, Shanta. Tendulkar on his own Terms. Madge V.M. *Vijay Tendulkar's*Plays*AnAnthology of Recent Criticism.* New Delhi: Pencraft International,2007.Print.

Grimke, Sarah. *Letters on the Equality of the Sexes and the Condition of Woman.*New York: Burt Franklin, 1970.Print.

Hutcheon, Linda. *Postmodernism and Feminism: Canadian Context.* Ed. ShirinKudechedkar. New Delhi: Pencraft International, 1995.Print.

Kanwar, Asha.*Ghashiram Kotwal: A Study Guide.* New Delhi: IGNOU, 1993.Print.

Omvedt, Gail. *We shall Smash This Prison: Indian Woman Struggle.* London:Zed Books, 1980.Print.

Rafia, M. H. Mohammed. "Women in Vijay Tendulkar's *Kamala*".*The Quest.*Vol.17.No2. 2. Decemeber, (2003): 63-65. Print.

Saran, Satya, and Vimal Patil."An Interview with Vijay Tendulkar, *Femina.*(June 8-22), 1984.37. Print.

Simon, Shibu. Man-Woman Relationship in the Plays of Vijay Tendulkar. *The Plays of Vijay Tendulkar Critical Explorations*.eds. Amar Nath Prasad, Satish Barbuddhe. NewDelhi:Sarup& Sons, 2008. Print.

Beauvoir, Simone de.*The Second Sex*. Trans. H. M. Parshley. London: Vintage Books, 1997. Print.

Tendulkar, Vijay. Kamala.*Five Plays*.Trans. Priya Adarkar. New Delhi: Oxford

University, Press, 1995.pp.1-52. Print.

Thankamma, Catherine. Women that Patriarchy Created: The Plays of Vijay Tendulkar,Mahesh Dattani and Mahasweta Devi. Madge V.M. *Vijay Tendulkar's Plays AnAnthology of Recent Criticism*. New Delhi: Pencraft International, 2007. Print.

Wadikar, Shailaja B. *Vijay Tendulkar A Pioneer Playwright*. New Delhi: Atlantic Publishers & Distributors (P) Ltd, 2008. Print.

6 *Sakharam Binder*: The Conflict between Powerful and Powerless

In Indian society, we have seen many customs and traditions that restrict human desires and expressions. On the name of customs, rituals and morality, women are strongly restricted and oppressed in various ways. In the second chapter of the present thesis, the researcher has studied how Vijay Tendulkar deals with the patriarchal society and exploitation of woman. He explores how a woman becomes a victim in the hands of men in the Indian urban middle-class society. The playwrightskilfully employs mock-court to reveal the patriarchal mind of Indian people. Tendulkar's fondness reflects when he bestows a voice to a woman in the male-dominated world in the form Leela Benare's monologue. Although patriarchy has no serious logic or rationality to support itself, yet patriarchal values are so enveloping that they are accepted and followed blindly by all human beings as universal truths.The play *Silence! The court is in Session* deals with the serious and bitter issue that unmarried motherhood.

Being a true believer of humanism, Vijay Tendulkar focuses entirely on the suffering and wretched condition of human beings. In this section of the thesis, the research's attempt is to study the play SKB which prominently sorts out the issue ofthe conflict between powerful and powerless. This issue is also related with feminism. So, it needs to undertake different sort of negotiation not only with the hegemonic power structure but also with one own choice of sexuality or gender.

Power is a central and integral part of the social system. A society is unimaginable without power and its relationships. Power comes and exercises at an interpersonal level. Being a social animal, man cannot live or create his existence in isolation. In the same way, a single person cannot exercise power and s/he require someone otherwise s/he becomes powerless.Individuals create a society and social functions in the form of a structure. MichelFoucault changed the concept of power by bringing it down to the plane of relations, and relation always needs more than one individual to exercise it. In this process, the individual who is an element of this social structure almost loses his individuality and identity

The concept of 'power' has been defined by many theorists. Neil Larsen, defines power asthat the wishes of those with more power will normally prevail over the wishes of those with less" (2). The definition clearly suggests that those who have power fulfill their wishes by using power over others or are powerless. Human beings have witnessed the conflict between powerful and powerless through class, gender, color, caste, and race throughout the centuries. The powerless or weak people have been governed, conquered, treated badly, and suppressed by powerful people.

Power is simply a capacity that assists in dealing with others. So, it directs that capacity may be unequal person to person and its effect that unequal relationship between those who employ power for their own purposes and those who are subject to its effects.In this sense, power may be used as an instrument of dominance. Professor Elaine Leeder also asserts, "Power is about control of the resource, ownership of the means of production, and the ability to control others, which comes from those who have historically been dominant" (54).

Power does play in an individual, a group, or a community to fulfill their purpose and to control others. Power can work out within the individual as a tool to show authority over the weak and powerless. Foucault illustrates power as "being conceived to be rational; something that is exercised from a variety of points in the social body rather than something that is acquired, seized, or shared. Relations of power are not considered to be secondary to other relationships—economic processes, knowledge relationships, sexual relations" (Smart 122).

We can find that there are highly individualized authority figures such as the king, the teacher, the priest, and the father who are allocated power and they use to control others. Sometimes they use freely for their interest and intention. When somebody gets or gains more power than others, it creates disharmony, struggle, or conflict in the society. Imbalance of power not only creates conflict between powerful and powerless people but also the violence in both.

If we observe the society, we get to know that Power is the root cause ofthe conflict between weak and strong. Power has different forms and levels butit finds in discriminations, it takes place verbal language, and it occurs in physical activities and at the mental level too. The conflict is a somehow inseparable part of a human relationship. It is an inevitable episode of disagreement that tends to occur between or within individuals. It is generated when one's values and beliefs regarding their historical, cultural and religious aspects are challenged. Most of the times conflicts happen between the powerful and the powerless.

Furthermore, conflicts also exist within each individual itself, even though the circumstances may vary in the case of every one of us. In other words, conflict is a matter that can be found between those in power states and those who have not. Those holding power feel superior and degrade whoever's inferior in their eyes—women, amongst the others. The conflict does not need to concern the existence of the power to occur, as it has evidently taken place amid the powerless.

Generally, power is supposed to exploit. It leads to abuse, classify, and divide along with prejudice. Power is also transferable and dynamic. These facts demonstrate power with the dominance/submission relationship implicit in reliance and the failure to differentiate oppression. Basically, power is used for persuasion or authority. So, sometimes it is either used to oppress or suppress others. In a very opposite way, it can be exercised to make coordination and centralization of group action by lawful authority to empower group members to achieve their goals. To follow groups' collective will, there must be a power structure through which group identity and goals are realized. The authority should not diminish feelings of the power of a group since it expresses a collective identity, not a perceived hierarchical difference in which members are subordinated.

Authority can be degenerated into intimidation, just as coercion can be transformed into authority. Authority is, therefore, also transferable. It is important to study how the changes take place in the power structure. It is also essential to recognize that the absence of power structures can be highly frustrating and harmful to social solidity and effective social unity. Power plays a very vital role in the universe. Man attempts to achieve it and exploits it for his benefit, neglecting its other aspects.

Radical feminists resist the idea that men exert power over and through women's bodies for their self-satisfaction. Radical feminists seek to revolutionarily overthrow the patriarchal order. They consider merely changing people's attitudes through liberalist recommendations of education are not enough to bring about a change in women's lives. They challenge liberal feminism, and their main goal is not to introduce equal rights (they do not want women to become like men) but to free women from all shackles of patriarchal society; the main challenge to patriarchy being in the form of separatism.

As we know, literature is a "system of representation" or "a mirror of society," and one of the functions of literature is to make people aware of social issues and contemporary situations. In the same way, it also represents powerful people as well as powerless people in a meticulous manner. Since the very beginning of human civilization, power, conflicts, and relationships have often been depicted in literature in various aspects. Many modern theories in general and feminist theories in particular study every social relationship. Feminism studies relationships in various dimensions to understand the conflicts.

Being a sensitive writer, Vijay Tendulkar exposes the relationship carefully in his plays. The playwright takes interest in this subject and projects in his plays. Imbalance of power not only creates conflict but also breaks the relation. Imbalance of power finds in individuals, groups, men and women, and their intimate kinship—marital, father-daughter, extramarital, as well as a blood relationship. Tendulkar has exposed the relationship between men and women as a relation between the exploiters and exploited. The playwright has exposed the bitter truth of women's exploitation due to the imbalance of power. It can happen through the relationship between wife and husband, a single woman and her fellows, and father and daughter in many of his plays.

We can easily detect the conflict between powerful and powerless in the plays of Vijay Tendulkar by a glance over the play. *Silence! The Court is in Session*, here is the conflict between an individual and society. Miss Benare is a middle-class woman wants to create her own identity by breaking the mundane rule of patriarchal society. The protagonist of*Ghashiram Kotwal* uses his daughter, Lalita Gauri as a tool with the intention to achieve power over the rival Brahmins of Poona. The conflict takes place between Gashiram and Nana Phadnavis. The play *Kamala* not only depicts the exploitation of powerless, a tribal woman, Kamala but also shows Jaisingh as a powerful journalist who also becomes powerless. Kamala and Sarita become victims in the hands ofpowerful and a career-minded journalist, Jaisingh Jadhav. The similar kind of incident is portrayed in the plays like *Vultures* and *Kanyadan*. In addition to the rivalry between men, *The Vultures* shows us how even a sister is physically and psychologically tortured by her authoritative brothers and how she lives submissive life as if a frightened bird. *Kanyadan*also has a similar theme. Nath wants to bring the change in society so he uses his own daughter's life. As a consequence, she is exploited and oppressed by the authority of her father and husband.

The play,*Sakharam Binder* (1972) also brings outcontroversy in Tendulkar's dramatic world. The play got popularity in Marathi as well as in other languages. It was first performed on stage in 1972 and was banned later around 1974 and has been translated by Kumud Mehta and Shanta Gokhale. The renowned playwright and critic, Girish Karnadapplauded the play SKB "the best play written in the last thousand years" (Renuka 4).Amid the immense controversy,*Sakharam Binder* has first performed three decades ago.

The Shiv Sena, the regional party of Maharashtra, strongly opposed the play.There are some cruxes of the controversy reflect in the form of the language, anti-Brahmin customs, illicit relationships, graphic depiction of violence and the explicit references to sex. The play was also criticized as being against the sacred institution of marriage. The matter was admitted in the High Court and the Court rejected the guidelines of the Censor Board. The ruling of the High Court proved a positive blow against censorship and the audience witnessed one of the most naturalistic plays of Indian theatre.

Being a stem feminist, Tendulkar breaks patriarchy and tries to give full of freedom and rights to women as well as men in the play. He shows a man-woman relationship in this perspective. The relationship is dealt with the imbalance of power. The women become helpless and powerless creatures due to an imbalance of power, and this imbalance comes from patriarchal monopolies. The play critically represents the unequal power between the male and female members of Indian society.

Sakharam Binder, the play deals with the conflict between powerful and powerless. The title itself suggests that the play may have one dominant figure, which is Sakharam, who represents his curious and complicated lifestyle. Like Shakespearean tragedy, Tendulkar gives the protagonist name to this play. Although the playwright does not portray the hero, who has high status and is a great tragic figure as we find in Shakespearean tragedies, there are some common similarities and traits.

Sakharam also reminds us of the of the anti-hero Jimmy Porter of John Osborne. He is a result of the social disinterest. Jimmy is an anti-hero because he lacks traditional heroic qualities and virtues. Obviously, he is not an ideal character. He intends to make his own world against the accepted social conventions. We can find similar qualities in the character of Sakharam.

Being a skilled dramatist, Tendulkar emphasizes more on character and is more conscious about the creation of character in the drama. Character is the kernel property of drama. Before writing plays, Tendulakar finds his characters in reality and then starts writing. In this context, he admits, "My characters are not cardboard characters; they do not spread my language; rather, I do not speak my language through them; they are not my mouthpieces; but each of them has his or her own separate existence and expression" (Agrawal 40-41).

The play is designed in three acts and deals with personal as well as interpersonal conflicts of the characters. Twelve scenes are included in the first act. Some scenes pass quite short in the play. There are no dialogues; only stage instructions and darkness regarding the visual to be presented in the third scene of the first act.

The man-woman relationship is the gist of the play. Being an expert playwright, Tendulkar shows us a desirable, vital, and useful end of reconstruction of the man-woman relationship. Tendulkar skillfully delineates a triangle of relationships among Sakharam, Laxmi, and Champa. Laxmi and Champa are respectively the seventh and eighth mistresses of Sakharam. He gives a challenge to the sanctified institution of marriage. Breaking the social tradition of marriage, he prefers to have a contractual relationship with women. He keeps his conditions and rules before each woman when he brings women.Sakharam sanctions the entry of women who accept his rules and conditions, including sexual relations. While gaining and using his authority, Sakharam forgets the basic nature of power and becomes a victim of it. It is very appealing to see how power plays and transfers from Sakharam to Laxmi and makes him powerless.

The first act opens with the entry of Laxmi into Sakharam's house as his seventh mistress. She cannot bear Sakaram's hot temper and excessive demands. Her life becomes pathetic and full of misery that results in the conflict between Sakharam and Laxmi. She tries to make him religious, soft, and domesticated up to a certain extent. But she cannot get success. Disappointed after her genuine attempts, she leaves Sakharam's house at the end of the first act.

The second act shows the entry of the eighth mistress, Champa. Being a sensuous, bold, and unconventional woman, Champa brings out a drastic change in Sakharam's life. This act depicts Sakharam's lust towards Champa, and it makes him passive. Here we find that Sakharam becomes powerless before her physical appearance and boldness. Hence, conflicts arise between Sakharam and Champa. Once again, he becomes drunkard to satisfy her pleasure. Laxmi returns back to Sakharam House at the end of the second act. It confirms that she is so weak to survive in the male-dominated world, and she does not have any alternative to coming back to Sakharam's house.

We witness the conflict among the three characters in the third act. The presence of both women, Laxmi and Champa, creates chaos and conflict in Sakharam's life. It shows a complex psychological effect on him. Sakharam intends to fulfill his desires by suppressing two women. As a consequence, the conflict takes place among three and transforms into the murder of Champa. On one hand, Sakharam is dissatisfied with Laxmi's coolness and religiosity, and on the other hand, Champa's powerful body, which can satisfy anyone, even a dog or a corpse after getting drunk, also disturbs him.

In the presence of Laxmi, it confirms that he becomes impotent in his sexual relationship with Champa. Baffled, Sakharam beats and orders Laxmi to leave his house. By using her evil mind, Laxmi discloses Champa's illicit relationship with Dawood to Sakharam so that she may get a permanent entry into his house. The sexual relationship between Dawood and Champa hurts a lot. Without thinking about consequences, Sakharam murders Champa in his rage.

Ironically, the play ends, and it is confirmed that once Sakharam was powerful and used to pride him; now he is powerless and helpless before Laxmi. She assists in hiding Champa's dead body to escape from the punishment of the law. Moreover, he is consoled by Laxmi and gets moral justification from her. We find a dramatic transformation in Laxmi from a cold-blooded conspirator to a powerful woman.

The play is also the representation of male domination, exploitation of women, sex, harassment, and violence. Tendulkar believes that violence is a device that sets in human nature. Due to power, violence takes place in various ways. To investigate the thread of conflict between powerful and powerless in this play, it requires studying man-woman relationships.

We may call these happenings cultural polemics, ideological debates, conflicts, or struggles, but at the deepest level, there is violence. Vijay Tendulkar regards violence positively as a source of energy. The play also generates very vital, progressive, and constructive social-cultural power out of theatrical usage of violence—particularly gender violence, which is a main source for the conflict. Tendulkar asserts, "Violence is something that has to be accepted as fact; it's no use describing it as good or bad. Projection of it can be good or badd... be turned into vital, useful, constructive transformative force; it depends upon you that how you use it or curb it at times" (Wadikar 90).

After the creation of a remarkable character, Sakharam Binder, a controversial wave raises in Tendulkar's career. He has occupied a place in the audience and readers' minds for a long time. Being an outcaste, he proudly lives his life alone. N.S. Dharna argues, "the important fury of a male masochist." He asserts, Vijay Tendulkar's Sakharam Binder is an exposition of the hypocrisy, jealousy, masochism, and lust of middle-class males (67).

Though Sakharam is not rich, being a man, he possesses masculine power. This masculine power reflects through his rude language, his deeds, and his all-over behavior. It hints us that he is not a common man but a man of tremendous power. This power has made him different from others. Being an extremely independent man, Sakharam's aloofness and vulgarity make him an exploiter of women. The use of power means exploitation of others. Sakharam directly suppresses women by bringing them into his house.

He could not bear the merciless beating of his father in childhood. He ran away from his home at the age of eleven after getting fed up with his father's beatings. It seems his weakness and helplessness. His unloving parents used the power and gave him the ill-treatment. That bitter experience of childhood life makes him a crude, extraordinary, and untraditionally powerful man.

He holds the power of termination of the contract and does not allow any freedom to the women. Both Laxmi and Champa come to learn that he is an absolute calculating, pitiless, drunkard, and sadist to boot. Sakharam Binder's outspoken and rude nature reflects many times in the play. He challenges society and criticizes openly people. His friend Dawood tries to make him aware to think about the people and his immoral way of life; he becomes irritated and angrily responds that:

> People! What do I owe them or their bloody fathers? Did they feed me when I went hungry? I lay dying in the Miraj Mission Hospital. Did anyone bother to find out whether I was alive or dead? Don't talk to me about people, Dawood.
>
> (Act 2. Scene 7.173)

Breaking the traditional path of marriage, Sakharam remains unwed his whole life. It proves his practical nature as well as his power to attack society. But why does he lead to an unmarried life? His decision to remain unmarried may have diverse and many reasons. One reason is to live free without taking any responsibility of a traditional Indian husband. A second reason is the lack of parental love or intimacy for him that results in his resentment towards the relationship and other people in his society. The third, he has disbelief in any permanent relationship. Commonly, we can understand or judge a person whether he is powerful or powerless by his action, behavior, and deeds. Powerful people always revolt against mundane life and the traditions. Sakharam rejecting the traditional path of marriage proves his power. The same Sakharam does in his life.

Sakharam makes a close relationship only with the weaklings and powerless women. He chooses the only suitable option for him. He selects the discarded, powerless, and helpless women so he gets an appropriate liaison to rule over them. He assures him that they can never overpower him. If they try to do so, he is free to discard them as per the condition. He affirms, "Everything comes to an end. So where's the point in getting involved? And involved with what? As long as one manages to be happy without doing anyone harm, that's about all" (Act 1. Scene 1.130). He, therefore, leaves those mistresses without any care or regrets. David G. Winter, a political psychologist, mentioned in one of his research papers that:

> Some of the concerns with power lead men to a profligate sexuality-for example, having sexual intercourse at an earlier age ... and with more partners. Such menseem drawn to the mythic figure of Don Juan, who seduced and abandoned women ("in Spain, already a thousand and three," according to the libretto for Mozart's opera Don Giovanni). Like Don Juan, moreover, these men seem to pursue sex not for its own sake, but rather as a way of demonstrating their power byexploiting, humiliating, and debasing women. For example, power-motivated men prefer dependent wives... who do not have independent careers... Notsurprisingly, such men are likely to turn violent with their intimate partners. (387)

The striking quality of Sakharam's character is his love for individualism and existence. He is totally against the established conventions of society. The same quality is found in the character of Leela Benare, who possesses free nature and liberty in *Silence! The Court is in session.* She wants to create her identity and individuality. But as a woman, she cannot rejoice in her authority and free spirit. Sakharam enjoys his liberty and free nature because he is a man. It concludes that gender discrimination and unequal treatment are certain to women and find everywhere in society.

That is one of the prime objectives of feminism. Tendulkar has very artistically portrayed this issue in his characters differently. We can see Tendulkar's sympathy towards Benare in STCIS Sarita and in Kamala in KML and Jyoti in KND. Their suffering is reflected with a fullness of compassion. It proves his bent of mind towards feminism, though he denies being a feminist.

Another most important characteristic of his personality is the presence of extreme bitterness for hypocritical people. He expresses, "I have yet to meet a more gutless breed than these husbands.We're a whole lot better than those swine!" (Act1.Scene1.129). Whatever he does, he does it for himself. Renuka's comment is quite significant in this regard: "Sakharam is frank and outspoken, and his rough idiom seems the right vehicle for the values he has evolved for himself. He tries to work out an independent philosophy of life with no false obligations "(25).

Sakharam brings women and warns them to act as his wives. He is not an emancipator by bringing powerless women but an "exploiter of women" and "powerful man." He never takes the responsibility to live his whole life with a single woman.Considering himself a powerful man, he provides shelter to powerless and helpless women. He uses a mask and fulfills his rude and egotistical deeds. He likes to use masculine power on weak women that create conflicts in his house. He makes to silence not only women like Laxmi and Champa but also children. He threatens, "Hey, you! What the hell's happening here? What's gaping at? You think we're dancing naked around here?" (Act 1. Scene, 1.125).

He treats women worse than their real husbands and tries to prove he is a greater man than their husbands. He always employs his liberty and power to throw away the withered, suppressed, and pined women so that he can bring new and comparatively younger ones. He loves to be free from all social bondage and enjoys every new bird. He does not like to continue his relationship with a single woman. His inhuman deed exposes that he is a powerful man.

His orthodox parents treated Sakharma badly. We see that deep wound in his opposite behavior. Naturalism highly reflects in his character. He uses vulgar language, drinks liquor, smokes cigars, and indulges in mechanical sex. He wants to be a ruler, so he brings helpless, powerless, and cast-off women for sexual and physical needs. He makes the rule of his house very clear: "This is not a royal palace. It is Sakharam Binder's house." Later, he tells a frightened Laxmi exultantly that "I have been like this right from birth. Born naked, I was. My mother used to say, He is a Maher born in a Brahmin home" (Act 1. Scene 1.127). According to V. M. Madge, "This opening harangue is a crucial part of the text in that it not only tells what sort of a man Sakharam is but also contains seeds of a dichotomy in his character, of which he is blissfully unaware" (121). Sakharam warns Laxmi and expects her to behave:

> I like everything in order here. Won't put up with slipshod ways. If youare careless, I shall show the door… I am the master here. …A house must be a home, you understand? (Act 1.Scene 1.125)

This verbal expression and the order show the authority of Sakharam. It also proves his exploitive nature like a king of his kingdom. Every time he orders women and accomplishes his pleasure. He remains deaf to the emotional and moral implications. Moreover, he justifies all his acts through claims of modern, unconventional thinking, and comes up with hollow arguments meant in fact to enslave women. He welcomes Laxmi in the house with his own tyrannical conditions in the first act.

> SAKAHARAM.Come in. Have a good look around. This house is like me. I won't have to complain later on. Yes, look carefully around the place. If you think it is all right, put down your bundle and stay. You'll get two Saris to start with, then one every year... There's a well at the back of the house... Well dries up in the summer...Then you'll have to fetch water from the river. ... I won't have you leaving the house unless there is work to be done.

His confession and instruction prove that he wants to impose his authority over a poor and wretched woman, Laxmi. He is very conscious of the discipline of home. With his masculine power, he rules over Laxmi and considers her as private property. Sakharam treats her as his wife without marriage. It indicates that he is fully aware of the status wife and a mistress. It exposes his male chauvinism. He warns:

> .... If someone calls, you're not supposed to look up and talk... If it's Stanger, you'll have to cover your head and answer him. .. Maybe I am a rascal, a womanizer, a pauper. Why maybe I am all that but I must be respected in my own house... I am the master here. What I say goes. Others must obey. No question should be asked. .. You'll have to be a wife to me... If you agree to deal? Right then, go and make some tea. ... If you live here, you don't need to fear anyone". (Act1.Scene1.125-126)

This confession of Sakharam Binder exposes his power, egoistic attitude, self-esteem, a sense of fear, his male chauvinism, and even self-hatred. He establishes male supremacy through his overprojection and assertion. He follows his contractual relationship as the celebration of monarchical authority. Surprisingly, he leads his whole life without marriage, but he gets everything. This disparity highlights in patriarchal culture where a woman cannot live alone and she must have the protection of a father, husband, or son; otherwise, she is considered a morally bad woman. For the sake of protection, women take Sakharam as a shelter and bear a lot. Benare is suffered and subdued because she is all alone in her life in the play *Silence! The Court is in session.*

Sakahram makes his rules like a tyrant, yet ironically, each woman is told that she is free to leave whenever she wants. But in reality, he compels women to give up his home. Using women's weakness, he makes himself powerful. He knows that his authority can impose on powerless women. Though he tries to show kindness by giving her a sari, 50 rupees, and a ticket to wherever she wants to go. Behind this emotional chapter, he wants to carry out his plan. His intention is to show the rules of Sakharam Binder. So nobody can break it.

The relationship between Sakharam and Laxmi is exposed in the play as likewise victimizer and victim, exploiter and exploited, master and slave, lord and subject, and importantly powerful and powerless. Their relationship raises conflict. Laxmi admits his behavior: "My orders have to be obeyed," as and when Laxmi complains against the wrongs done to her: "I've never heard a kind word here.

Always barking orders, curses, and oaths and threatening to throw me out. Kicks and blows. There I was in agony after I'd been belted, and all you wanted me to do was laugh." (Act 1. Scene 9.148). This juncture shows her mental agony and physical exploitation at the hands of Sakharam. It also implies his manipulation of power, and that drives conflict. She bears all things mutely because she is weak in various ways. Though she is subjected to rigorous exertion, she quietens her deep voice for a year, fearing to throw out of the house. At last Laxmi bursts out:

> You think I am afraid to tell you? How much more can a person bear? It's a year now since I entered this house. I haven't had a single day's rest. Whether I'm sick or whether it's a festal day. Nothing but work, work; work all the time. You torture me thewhole day, you torture me at night. I'll drop dead one of these days and that will be the end. (Act 1. Scene 9.146)

Laxmi raises her voice against the authority of Sakharam. She has her values and wants to lead her life in her own way. Laxmi tries to defend herself, and it feels insecure in Sakharam's mind. The conflict raises, a quarrel takes place in their relationship, and their relationship comes to an end for a short time. He fears that he may lose power because Laxmi tries to lift up her voice against the authority of Sakharam.

> LAXMI. And you beat me in return. And cursed me and tortured me.
>
> SAKHARAM. Then what did you expect me to do? Be your salve and lick your feet?
>
> LAXMI. You'll know that once I am gone.
>
> SAKHARAM. Then why don't you go? When you're forced to lead a dog's life, you'll come to your senses." (Act1. Scene 9.148)

Sakharam discards Laxmi because she disobeys his rules. Here also we get to know that she starts overlooking his lusty advances and imposes her values on Sakharam. So, he shows the way of withdrawal. Moreover, Sakharam, the womanizer, has become habitual of having sex with different women. Laxmi is unable to provide him any substitute for a hotwoman.It is evident that a woman's survival and happiness under a patriarchal order largely relies on the whims and wishes, desires, and dictates of man.

He signifies the double standards of patriarchy. Under the aspect of helping the women in suffering and distress, he indirectly uses them as a toy of sex. It is evident that the women were trapped by circumstances into living a coarse and brutalized life with Sakharam. They have no economic independence, so they face miserable conditions. It evidences his practical and double-standard nature when he finds that Laxmi lacks that spark from her body and tries to rule over him. He warns her, "Don't ever come again to his house. Just go your way. Go, find someone who'll feed you and put up with all your queenly airs. Go and live with him" (Act 1. Scene 9.149). It also indicates his escapism from the role of husband and his power that throws away Laxmi of the house.

Dawood is also an important character in the play. He is a Muslim and friend of Sakhram. His presence at Ganesh Pooja is strongly objected by Laxmi. Saying that Dawood "is a Muslim—and we are Hindus." Here conflict takes place, and Sakharam fails to rage his control. On hearing religious discrimination, Sakharam scolds and slaps her. This incident reveals that Sakharm is not against Laxmi but against all those conventions that create disharmony in society. This conflict shows that though Laxmi was frail, helpless, and powerless before Sakharam, she could also use her power by showing religious ethics. She strongly opposes, "If you want to beat me, beat me inside. Not in front of God! He's only come to the house today" (Act 1. Scene 6.144). Sakharam is by birth a Brahmin, and Laxmi considers her a wife of Sakharam, so she is also a Brahmin. This scene shows that she exercises her power of the upper caste on the lower caste or the weak to humiliate Dagwood. This is nothing but the demonstration of power relationships to control the subaltern class of people.

In this context, Sakharam appears an idealist who cannot bear any discrimination in the name of religion, but on the other hand, he slashes Laxmi. It proves his domination, cruelty, violent nature, power, and urges to dominate. Sakharm assaults Laxmi in this incident. It reminds us of the story of Mahatma Gandhi's idealism and humanism. He had done the same with his wife, Kasturba Gandhi, when she denied cleaning the toilet as part of his ideas of the removal of inequity. Here Tendulkar shows two different views of Sakharam. He is a great idealist who treats

Muslim friends equally at the same time and shamelessly beats her by using his authority, showing his unkindness.

This conflict between Laxmi and Sakharm also shows when somebody tries to impose values and principles in others life, it rises conflict. This incident also proves that she might look frail and withered, is not dead inside. She can also use her religious power and stand up for what she thinks right and believes in. No matter how bad Sakharam beats her, she sticks to her stance. Another thing is also perceivable here that Laxmi is so religious. She still believes in religious activities and those values give her powerin her helplessness condition. Though Laxmi is thrown out by her husband and Sakharam Binder, her power, determination and courage come across the event that takes place in Act Three.

Laxmi forgets her own identity and leads a passive life with Sakharam. She is a simple, straightforward, and even plain woman. Therefore, nobody could probably claim her as evil-minded and having been deserted to her husband. This simplistic yet clear-cut distinction makes Laxmi feel very righteous and lets her consider herself as a chaste woman. At last, both of them jointly leave in a very good manner. Undoubtedly, her departure left a deep impact on Sakharam. He confesses, "There have been many women here, but this one left a mark before she went away" (Act 1 Scene 12.153).

Sakharam never vacillates to criticize orthodox upper caste moralist conceptions of family, marriage, caste, religion, etc. And at the same time, we can seek a double standard in Sakharam. It exposes the so-called upper caste social reformation as well as radical anti-family positions prevailing in society. Though both appear opposite, they are two sides of the same coin. Women are exploited in both conditions. They are anti-woman and male-dominated ideas. It is a clear example of gender violence where women become victims in the hands of a male.

Sakharam considers that morality is only a selfish means and chooses private morality against the expectations of public morality. To deceive others, people are deceived by themselves also. Sakharam also exploits women, but one day he is exploited and becomes a victim of circumstances. The entire phenomenon of deception turns into a kind of social contract. According to Sakharam people, "put on an act all the time" and follow the formula, "You hold your tongue and I'll hold mine!"... "If you live here, you don't need to fear anyone. This Sakharam Binder—he is a terror. He is not scared of God or of God's father" (Act 1. Scene 1. 126).This directs that Sakharam considers himself like a mighty god, and he uses it to dumb the women. When the same kind of process and lewdness increases and continues for a long time in a society, people accept the devious behavior as the normal practice. This general process of mutual hypocrisy distresses and humiliates only the weak. The patriarchy is an appropriate example in which women are conditioned to accept the domination of men. He wants to show his superiority over others and enjoys his life in his own way. On the one hand, Sakharam discloses how he is different from others. He admits:

> Everything comes to an end. So where is the point in getting involved and involved with what as one manages to be happy, without doing anyone any harm, that's about all. But—no dishonesty allowed. If you sin – you must be ready to slap your face and, 'yes, I sinned 'you must ready to the tap. (Act 1 Scene1.130)

As far as Sakharam is concerned, he treats and uses his women as if they are his private goods. He imposes his masculine power over the women. As a result, it creates conflict between master and slave. He strives to master the whole being. He rebukes, I'll knock out your teeth if I hear that again! I'm offering you tea from my cup, and you tell me yours is in the kitchen" (Act 1. Scene 4.137). He possesses exceptional strength of will and leads a life of a hedonist that airs him the supreme importance. It also demonstrates his authority over a weak woman.

By not permitting women to have any kind of intimacy with anybody else while living in his house, Sakahram snatches the basic freedom of wretched women. We can see Laxmi has an illusionary friendship with ants and crows. He warns Laxmi not to talk to ants, sparrows, and cows. He threatens her, "What the hell's going on here? Is this a house or a loony-bin? Remember what I told you? Don't you dare repeat this sort of thing! All madness must stop at once. I'll knock your brains out, I will" (Act 1. Scene 4.139).

The fifth scene is a short one, but it is important because it shows Sakharam's mighty power and gives an insight into his mind. Laxmi's laughing at an ant feels annoyed and makes him insecure, so he forcefully asks her to laugh for himself too: "Get up and laugh. Laugh or I'll choke the life out of you. Laugh! Laugh! Go on, laugh!" (Act1.Scene5.141). The wild laughter of Laxmi grips his consciousness, and it assumes the form of obsession. He feels the loss of his masculine power, so he compels to laugh the same way as she laughed in the company of Ant. Although she laughs at the compulsion of Sakharam, Laxmi's wild laughter seems like a kind of revolt against his authority.

Laxmi passively accepts the conditions of Sakharam for getting the protection from outside the world. She is the embodiment of the ideal Indian womanhood—poor, loyal, docile, religious, self-effacing, tender-hearted, etc. She uses her loyalty and religiosity to gradually change Sakharam's house into a family. She starts with God and worship and thus attempts to bring some change in Sakharam's life. Her religious power tries to change the mind of Sakharam and dominate him. Religion plays a vital role in Laxmi's life. Hence, she uses it not only to protect herself but also to impose on other lives of individuals.

But at the same time, some changes take place. Sakharam, who was deprived of enjoying the status of Swami, or God of woman, unconsciously feels happy about these developments. Earlier he never thought of God, but due to Laxmi, he gradually turns religious; for example, he starts taking a regular bath, performs Pooja, etc., almost like a family man. It demonstrates that Laxmi gets success to bring out changes in Sakharam. It also indicates she imposes her religious power on Sakharam.

Laxmi's submissive nature and simple living style, in addition to her religious leanings, force Sakharam to give up his power as a master and his negative capabilities. She is not ready to leave his house. She says, "I stayed here for a whole year. This house became my home. And now again. It is a bad thing to be so attached... I won't be seeing you again... I gave it all I had. I kept nothing back" (Act 2. Scene 9.153). The conflict between Sakharma and Laxmi takes place frequently. Sometimes

Sakharam beats and forcefully sex her. As a result, she feels that she is unable to bear the sufferings as a mistress.

Finding this chance, Sakharam gets rid of her as he feels disgusted with the monotonous presence of Laxmi. He might be cruel, but he prefers a liberal mind. He accepts that Laxmi has every right to opt for her choices in the same way he maintains his own autonomy. On the other hand, Laxmi lacks the essential sensuality and thus finds herself unable to fulfill his physical demands and is therefore unable to leave. According to Shailaja B. Wadikar:

> Laxmi fails to fulfill his excessive physical lust and Sakharam remains blind to her expectations. Both cannot satisfy each other either physically or psychologically. There is no sharing, no harmony in their relationship; their life is totally disrupted. At last, they part company, saying good-bye to each other in good humor and a very cordial manner. (3)

Laxmi is a great example of Indian womanhood who gazes at the person like Sakharamas her God. Like Sarita in KML, Laxmi endures all suffering get her in Sakhram house. Here lies the crux of the conflict between these two apparently contrasting characters.Sakharamwarns Laxmi to "stop your yelling. Enough is enough.We aren't married. There's nothing to bind us. We don't need to remain tied to each other. You can go your way. I can go mine" (Act 1 Scene 10.151).

The womanizer, Sakharam, always chooses a safety device of the contractual relationship for him. When Laxmi is thrown away, her empty space is immediately occupied by a new 'bird', Champa, who is younger and more attractive than Laxmi. She is an idle, arrogant woman. For the first time in his life, Sakharam has the tables reversed on him, and we find that Sakharam is an absolute powerless in the hands of Champa.

Sakharam never thinks about the pleasure or the pain of his partner and rudely forces her to have sex with him even against her desires. It is his weapon of manly power and authority that is frequently employed by him to suppress the women. The vice of the womanizer suggests his individuality and privilege over weaklings that raise conflict between powerful and powerless.

As usual, he dictates his rules to Champa as soon as she enters the house. When Sakharam mentions rules to Champa, she takes lightly:

CHAMPA.Looks too old to me.

SAKHARAM. {now in control}. If you don't like it, you can go out... I'm famished. Is there anything to eat? ...... You'll find something in the kitchen.

CHAMPA {sits down}. Then why don't you go and have a look? (Act

She seems to be assured that she should not get scared of anything. She counters Sakharam by saying: "Scared? Who, me? And Scared of whom? My husband? (Spits) What can he do to me?" (157). Although Champa accepts the contract of Sakharam, she does not surrender herself to Sakharam. She accepts her own choices rather than the commands of others. She lives not to like to accept the interference of others. So far Champa is concerned her own authority is important and in which there is no space for the terror and power of Sakharam.

Champa finds to be different from other women who were deserted by Sakharam. She is straightforward not to lose her own temper, identity, freedom, and choice. Here Sakharam seems powerless before Champa's charm and dominating nature. It also reveals that Sakharam's authority has now been transferred to Champa. Most often, Vijay Tendulkar's female characters are projected as passive, submissive, and having a tendency toward endurance. They are seldom assertive or rebellious. But this particular woman, viz. Champa, rules and dominates others.

Champa orders to Sakharam"You mean me? But I've never made tea in all my life... In my husband's house, my mother-in-law used to make it, and, at home, my old man used to make the tea and cook the food" (Act 2. Scene 1.58). It observes that Sakharam cannot rule over her like previous women. His power is transformed to Champa.

After enjoying tea and paan, she is tired, wants to go to bed. Sakharam does not like her sleeping arrangements but he finds helpless under these circumstances. The conflict between both of them shows Champa's power and also her rigid behavior:

CHAMPA. I shall sleep for an hour or so.

SAKHARAM. But it is still day!

CHAMPA. So what? Just remember to wake me when the food is ready. Is not there a cot here? Or a mattress?

SAKHARAM. No.

CHAMPA. What kind of a home is this?

SAKHARAM. And you shall have to make the food yourself. That is a woman's job and woman must do their own jobs. That is the rule around here.

CHAMPA. Rule! Is this a school or a court or something?

SAKHARAM. A rule is a rule. If you do not like it, out you go.

CHAMPA. (loud yawn) I am so sleepy. (Act 2.Scene 1.161)

Being a powerful woman and an extremist, Champa challenges the authority of Sakharam and condemns male chauvinism. It is confirmed that, like other women, she is not passive and sufferer but a powerful ruler. Here Tendulkar exposes Champa as a strong woman, which indicates his radical feminist approach. It also breaks down the discrimination between men and women that is the goal of feminism.

Sakharam, as usual, expects that Champa maintains the rules of his home, but his hollow expectations were broken when Champa entered his home. She possesses exceptional sensual beauty that attracts Sakharam passionately. Even she ridicules the false authority of Sakharam. Champa enjoys her power of beauty over Sakharam and Dawood. Instead of making tea for herself, Champa orders Sakharam to prepare tea. The interaction of Sakharam and Champa proves that Sakharam feels insecure, and therefore, he fails to tolerate appreciation for Dawood.

He would not allow her to speak to Dawood. He dictates that "in this house, I won't allow too much talking to strangers." When she is about to change her sari in the living room, he says, "Not here. Do all that in the kitchen when Dawood comes out." But she cannot hesitate to change the sari in the presence of Dawood. She declares, "What's there to be so shy about if I'm going to stay here?" (Act 2. Scene 1.160).

She rules over everyone who comes into her contact. When she feels hungry, she asks Sakharam to find something for eating. She would ask Dawood to bring a nice pan with tobacco. Baffled with her reckless behavior, Sakharam humbly pleads for the acknowledgment of his mastery over the house. He realizes her dominating power.

Champa's physical charm captivates Sakharam, and it provides power, cruelty, and aggression to her. Sakharam is infatuated by her personality, as he was never before with any other woman. This is the cause to shift his power to Champa. In the encounter with Laxmi, Sakharam proves his power, and he never confirms an established ideology. But in the counter of Champa, he survives gender-specific roles.

Dawood reminds Sakharam of the olden days when "Laxmi bhabhi was there." Sakharam gets enraged at the mention of her name in his house and says, "Laxmi's gone. She's dead as far as I'm concerned... Now it's Champa. Nothing else. Nobody can match her little finger. You don't know what fun Champa is" (Act 2. Scene 7.173). Sakharam appreciates Laxmi and reveals that he has lost his hallow nature and power.

Champa, unlike Laxmi, is an irreligious woman. Living her life on her wish specifies bold female character.She believes in herself, not in religious deeds and God. The chief cause of conflict is that Champa lacks domestic qualities also. Therefore, he scolds her for being drunk, untidy, and dirty on a religious holiday.

> Drunk so early in the morning? What is so wrong with you? This is not night. Champa, you should not drink on a holy day like Dassera. On a holy day, the woman of the house should look all clean and tidy. (Act 2. Scene 8.174)

Sakharam, who has kept his women as his private property, has mastered their whole being and has hitherto led the life of a hedonist, but Champa alters him as a passive and negligible one. Although she seems apparently "gross and sensual, she, too, is touchy and sensitive to some of the issues of life" (Wadikar 3). She is not ready to be letexploited sexually by

Sakharam. She refuses his amorous advances boldly on the first night. She rebukes Sakharam: "I don't like it at all that man-woman stuff. I had my honor to save "(Act 1. Scene 1.62). But after drinking alcohol, she accepts to have sex.

Champa does not admit Sakharam as her husband, as Laxmi has accepted by wearing mangalsutra (the wedding ornament that married Hindu women wear around their neck). "Look at this. I wore this in his name. I belong to him. If I have to be kicked, let him kick me; if I have to die, let me die in his lap—in full glory like a married woman" (Act 2. Scene 3.187).Wearing mangalsutra suggests that Laxmi follows the orders of Sakharam like a wife, but Champa, on the other hand, denies and imposes her orders on Sakharam. Champa shows her power strongly over Sakharam.

When we juxtapose both women, Laxmi and Champa, we find the dissimilarity in each other. Laxmi is a religious, submissive, and devoted woman. Champa is irreligious, sturdy, and sensuous. She is also an aggressive woman. She is younger than Laxmi. Sakharam is captured by her body structure. He impenitently speaks about the sexual appetites that he "couldn't fix my mind on work...Last night... It was great fun. All day I could think of nothing else" (Act 2. Scene 5.170). His friend Dawood also likes her figure. Sakharam is so bewitched. Even he begins to skip even his daily work at a press. Formerly, she was the wife of the policeman, Faujdar Shinde. Her husband was impotent, so she herself abandoned her frail, drunkard, and impotent husband, Fauzdar Shinde. But Laxmi's case is different. She was deserted by her husband because she could not produce a child.

The master of his house, Sakharam, is found helpless before Champa in the course of the play. It is the cause of the conflict between Sakharam and Champa. He reminds Champa that "you were in the streets when I picked you up. I fed you... Champa: I will wake up the whole place; I tell you. I can't bear it anymore." After his association with her becomes impotent, she objects to his approach: "I don't mind as long as you were a man. I won't take you now." (Act 3.Scene 5.193) and she takes recourse to Dawood. She "straightens all his curves," and he is sometimes helpless before her.

Power brings vices in a man like mischief, ugliness, hypocrisy, and immorality. We can find near about all vices in Sakharam Binder. His hypocrisy is easily seen when he condemns women who worship their husbands as gods. He, therefore, suggests Laxmi beat them (such husbands) with a slipper in public. Ironically here in the play, when Champaannoyes punches, humiliates, and abuses her husband by calling him by derogatory terms such as an impotent corpse whom all try to make a whore out of her every other time. Sakharam tries to stop Champa by telling her that "he is your husband. Haven't you a heart?" (Act 2.Scene 2.167).This incident proves that he feels the insecurity of his condition, power, and future.

On the surface level, Sakharam's masculinity seems to be strong, but internally he is weak and cowardly. It is his inward cowardice that finds an outlet into violence, unkindness, ugliness, and corruption. Furthermore, he murders Champa in rage at the end of the play. It proves his envious and criminal mind. He also feels insecure about his authority. The murder also reveals a bitter truth about Laxmi's plan to throw Champa out of the house. The murder of Champa raises several questions in the audience's mind. Why does Sakharm kill Champ? Why not Laxmi? Such questions remain without any perfect conclusion.

Critics take various stands regarding the murder of Champa. Actually, before the murder of Champa, there is a strong conflict between Laxmi and Sakharam, so we can expect that Sakharam should kill Laxmi, but he murders Champa in rage. We can also conclude that he feels irritated when he hears about Champa's illicit relationship, so he kills, or he wants to be king forever in his home, so he kills. That may be true because Champa is more powerful than Sakharam in many respects.

In his plays, Tendulkar reveals disharmony in spite of harmony in the relationship between man and society and man and woman. Owing to the inequality of power in societal structure, conflict arises between men and women. The stance of Tendulkar is of the detached observer while rendering Sakharam's powerful nature and weaknesses of women. Still, one can notice his leaning towards the victims of circumstances. He is far from being a shallow, hollow, and cheap entertainer, as he conscientiously depicted the predicament of women in the plays.

He dexterously portrayed Sakharam's character to indicate that power cannot give us everything he wants. Though Sakharam shows his powerful and dominating nature, he is helpless and powerless at the end of the play. This is the true nature of power. It cannot be exercised for a long time and it is generally shifted from one hand to other hands. He fulfills his sexual desire, but he remains alien in his entire life. He kills Champa but loses her beauty. He makes rules, but nobody accepts and follows. He lives life without satisfaction.

By imposing restrictions on women, such as preventing them from freely talking to a stranger or going outside and expressing their desire, Sakharam imposes his authority on women, and it creates the conflict. Sakharam warns, "And look. I won't have you leaving the house unless there's work to be done, you understand? If someone calls, you're not supposed to look up and talk. If it is a stranger, you'll have to cover your head and answer him briefly." (Act 1. Scene 1.126)

Actually, he fails to understand the nature of power—that it always gets transformed. Laxmi is powerless at the beginning and bears everything, but at the end the entire situation is reversed, and again Sakharam falls victim to the conflict and power. We can call this a tragic flaw in Sakharm's character. Marlowe's Dr. Faustus is one of the best examples of a tragic flaw. The tragic flaw in the character of Dr. Faustus is his ambitious nature. Faustus forgets that power has certain limitations. The same power proves the cause of his ruin.

A man-woman relationship is based on social structure. A man may enjoy different rules and status, and a woman suffer from the rules and traditions. Here Sakharam enjoys masculine power. The imbalance of power in a man-woman relationship is a determining factor in the status of man and woman. It is as old as the history of humanity itself.

Woman's predicament is one of the major aspects of Tendulkar's plays. His plays deal with the helplessness of women against society and men. The picture of women's lives in his plays is dark and exploitative. Here it is essential to analyze the powerless aspect, which strongly marks the character of Laxmi. She plays a crucial role not only in the life of Sakharam but also in the life of Champa. She is actually around a character that sufficiently surprises the reader through the play. In the beginning, she seems to be weak, mild, and passive, but in the end, she becomes a strong, courageous, and powerful woman that gains a permanent place in Sakharam's life. She does not only stand by Sakharam but also protects him from legal punishment.

The conflict took place between Laxmi and her husband. She was abandoned by her husband because she could not have a child. She is a victim of patriarchal gender stereotypes constructed about "true womanhood" or femininity. A woman who can produce children is considered a pious in the patriarchy. On the other hand, a woman who does not conceive is considered powerless, cursed, and unfruitful. Therefore, the family is regarded as a basic unit of progeny in the Indian context. The family is a root cause for women's suffering. If a woman could not produce a child, she is considered useless. In such a hideous situation, either she is discarded from family or she is left to live as a nun. She can be thrown out by her husband. It proves that there exists a moral and religious sanctity for it. In this context, Laxmi seems to be powerless because she lacks the power of reproduction and becomes a victim of gender stereotypes.

There is no evidence of any physical or sexual violence committed by her husband to Laxmi. So it is very difficult to digest that woman can be abandoned on the basis of her being unable to produce a child. It is such a stigma on society and mental degradation that results into women's exploitation. Moreover, women themselves are resopnisible to their exploitation. They learn and somehow easily accept these anti-woman values right from their childhood. It is this psychological makeup that must have a definite violent and negative stigmatic impact over Laxmi. As a result, she considers as weak and becomes helpless, powerless, and timid having least self- esteem in a male-dominated world

Champa, on the contrary, deserted her husband because he was impotent and unable to give her a child. In both, the cases thus physical power plays a meaningful role. It is linked with impotence and the cause to give up either wife or husband. Catherine Thankamma appropriately comments that "Laxmi is thrown out of her house by her husband but she still considers him her God. Champ, on the other hand, is a figure of revolt" (8).These two women characters thus are in direct contrast to each other. Laxmi accepts being a powerless and becomes a symbol of surrender while Champa is a symbol of revolt. She considers herself being powerful woman and rebels against the masculine world. Ironically, the common factor of their presence in Sakharam's house is impotency and physical weakness. Here we find male impotency and female impotence.

As mentioned, Sakharam doesn't believe in family or the institution of marriage. However, Laxmi's piousness and loyalty compel him to develop a slight change in his behavior and lifestyle. For Laxmi, he is her husband, and therefore she passively accepts him to be her master. Surprisingly enough, Laxmi is a slave who would teach the master. It is quite clear that though men may ill-treat women as badly as instruments of pleasure; women too also contribute to their own exploitation and violence.

Laxmi looks like an like an apparently powerless and weak woman, but as an ideal Indian wife, she knows how to use her power, having the armor of religiosity, passivity, and timidity over the over the overangry young man, Sakharam. She tries to bring some changes in patriarchs like Sakharam and transforms him into a responsible husband. It is after Laxmi's efforts that Sakharam feels some changes in him. He admits,Haven't I been less this year? Eh? Not that I don't drink now then, but isn't it much less? Tell me. Last month I had *ganja* just twice. And don't I do my... I bathe every morning" (Act 2. Scene 9.148). This change suggests that Laxmi also exercises her power to mold Sakharam. But being a man, he does not openly give any credit to Laxmi for such changes.

Sakharam ultimately likes Laxmi's religiosity, behavior, gesture, posture, etc. Laxmi's sexual appeal is basically that of an ideal wife. His magnetism is towards her or towards all abandoned housewives.Assuming husband as a God, he basically longs for such passive, powerless, virtuous women. He is fully aware that the house is the place where he can exercise his power at his will. This further indicates that despite his all radical claims, Sakaram really wants a woman who is already burned in patriarchal values of the family, but she should replace her husband from the throne and now be powerless and helpless.

When Laxmi comes back in a pitiable condition to Sakharam's house after a short stay in her nephew's house in Amalner, we see Champa's humanity. Laxmi is determined never to leave Sakharam's house now, but Sakharam does not want to have Laxmi back in the house. But Champa comes to Laxmi's rescue and proposes that she should do all the household work, and she herself would look after Sakharam's other needs. This similar idea, we find in the play *Kamala*, where Kamala makes a similar proposal to Sarita for a living, continues in the house of Jai Singh.

By accepting this proposal, Sakharam seems to be merciful. But it does not mean that Sakharam has changed his basic nature and become compassionate and considerate towards women. Here he finds a golden opportunity to rule over two women, and they will cater to his all sorts of needs and desires. It is evident that males, of course, would like to have the opportunity where two females would try to please the male and fulfill all his wishes.

The brutal murder of Champa not only finds us of violence and power on women but also exposes the hypocrisy and hollowness of the system where women are punished and men go scot-free for the same offense or sin. The same situation finds in play: silence. *The Court is in session.* Prof. Damle remains absent in the court, and Benare is harassed and punished by a male-dominated society. Sakharam scorns and abhors the institution of marriage and now gets indulged in contractual living-in by the convenience with destitute women.After killing Champa in rage, the despot Sakharam is seen bewildered and lost. He turns religious and tame in the company of Laxmi.

Two different facets of women's character come into direct quarrel and conflict. The simultaneous presence of Lakshmi and Champa brings psychological turmoil and results in temporary impotence. His aggressive boastfulness proves a mask of a powerful man. But actually, he is a victim at the hands of others. In alienation, Sakahram is treated like filth outside and 'othered' everywhere. In childhood, he was a victim of oppressive heterosexual patriarchal violence, and thus he projects his self-victimization onto women in his life. His masculinity is a regressive force that is inclined to violence and corruption and to rule over the powerless. His insecurity of authority not only culminates in Champa's murder but also discloses his inner self as a lonely and alienated human being.

There is a desire latent in the human psyche to gain power for self-respect. Champa turns all mastery of Sakharam into slavery. She has left her husband as she could not bear disgusting treatment. She tells Laxmi, "I put up with quite a lot. I can tell you that. But when I couldn't take it any longer, I turned my back on him and walked out" (Act 3.Scene 1.181). As we can see, she hardly pays attention to the speech of Sakharam after she enters his house. She baffles Sakharam with her reckless behavior, and he meekly pleads for the recognition of his mastery over the house. She allows Laxmi to stay in the house against his orders and argues with him:

> SAKHARAM. How dare you boss over me?
>
> CHAMPA.So? Are you going to beat me?
>
> SAKHARAM. I will when the time comes.
>
> CHAMPA. We will wait till the time comes. Meanwhile, drink your tea. It's getting cold (Act 3.Scene 2.185).

When in a fit of rage Sakharam murders Champa and is subject to capital punishment, Laxmi has her scheme ready. When Sakharam realizes that killing Champahe has committed an act of gross criminality, all his 'bravado' gets punctured. He frightens like a baby—"murdered——I've murdered her—murder—I've murdered" (Act 3.Scene 7.196). At this juncture, Laxmi grabs a better prospect for her future. Champa's death opens a new episode of possibilities for Laxmi. She gets a position to exert power over him; that is her inner desire. Laxmi comes forth and takes the initiative:

> Hush! Don't shout. Not a word. (Continue staring at the lifeless Champa.)Anyway, she was a sinner. She'll go to hell. Not you. I've been a virtuous woman. My virtuous deeds will see both of us through. I'll stay with you. I'll look after you. I'll do what you say. And I'll die with my head on your lap. Yes. Now don't be afraid. We'll-we'll bury her. (Act 3.Scene 7.196-197)

Apparently, she is a weak and powerless but inwardly she is a strong woman. Just as she proved the savior of his spiritual life before, now she proves the savior of his physical life. This event reveals her rebellious nature and incapacity of Sakharam. She speaks:

> We'll - we'll bury her. Where do you think? Not out there - no. Somewherehere. Inside and we'll say that she went away. No one will suspect. I'll swear by God. He knows everything. He knows I am virtuous. He'll stand by me. He won't judge you. I'll tell him to count my good deeds as yours. I'll do everything for you. (Act 3.Scene 7.196-197)

The conflict between Sakharam and Laxmi and Sakharam and Champa is due mainly because of Sakharm's obstinacy and bossism towards Laxmi and Champa. He could not satisfy Champa's animal desires. Due to contrast, the characters fall victim to one another. In other words, Sakharam is hurled between two forces. One is the spiritual revival that Laxmi attempts to bring about in him, and the other wants fulfillment of an animal desire that Champa demands from him and discards him afterward for his failure. Arundhati Banerjee remarks:

> The presence of Laxmi and Champa at the same time has a strange effect on Sakharam as if the two different strands in his character come into direct confrontation, creating a psychological turmoil in him and resulting in his temporary impotence (Banerjee. xiv-xv).

We find Sakharam bewildered after killing Champa. The intention of killing Champa is unclear. Actually, strong conflict takes place in Laxmi and Sakharam, but the result is Champa's murder. It is obscure to understand. It is obvious that he has lost the power of his wit due to the influence of these two forces.

Laxmi bears the injustice done to her by her husband as well as Sakharam. She is unreasonably thrown out of the house by her husband and pushed out by Sakharamas; she could not bear his brutality. Champa too is treated despicably by her impotent husband and so is forced to leave only to seek shelter under another equally savage man. As the second man, Sakharam too proves impotent. She turns indifferent to him and turns to yet another man, which eventually brings doom.

Tendulkar portrays the common oppositions of the suppressed human beings who attempt to find for themselves a comparatively free space. The play reveals how people victimize each other even though they are themselves subject to the same kind of victimization. Laxmi, who is portrayed as an ideal Indian woman like Savitri for her religiosity and devotion to Sakharam, turns out to be iniquitous for her own adherent. Although she and Champa mutually agreed to have a division of labor, Laxmi initially accepted the agreement as she was too helpless to oppose anybody; nonetheless, she keeps grudging against Champa for supplanting her place. The same kind of feeling begins to emerge in Champa. She notices some change in Sakharam because of Laxmi's presence.We can find some kind of psychological association between Sakharam's Mridanga and the presence of Laxmi in the house. Beena Agrawal comments, "the music produced by Mridanga ... is used to project the internal crisis of Sakharam by the playwright" (89). When Laxmi returns, he starts beating mridanga which makes Dawood come to his house: "Heard the mridanga, and I felt as if the old days had returned. . . . When you had the other bird—Laxmi(Act 3.Scene 4.185-186). Because of Laxmi and because of their mutual infatuation, an amorous relationship between Champa and Dawood develops and Champa begins to resist Sakharam's approaches-"Stop that 'Champa—Champa—' you're not a man—not since she came. She's made an impotent ninny of you. . . . You turn into a corpse—a worm" (Act 3.Scene 5.193).

In response to his aggression, Laxmi reveals Champa'sconnection with Dawood. In a way, both of the women represent the distinctive sides of feminine consciousness. Laxmi considers Champa sinful for exerting her authority on others and for her being unfaithful to the men she has been associated with. According to Mohan R. Limaye:

> Who deserted who is very important for Laxmi. In fact, it is the chief criterion on which she judges questions of marital fidelity. This is the basis on which she distinguishes her case from that of Champa, the second paramour of Sakharam. ... In the eyes of Laxmi, Champa is immoral because she has deserted her husband. Nobody could accuse Laxmi of having deserted her husband. (138-139)

Tendulkar unveils physical power through an impotent man and woman. Until Shinde was a policeman and was physically strong, everything went smoothly. Champa leaves her husband after realizing the weakness of her husband.Champa calls her husband an impotent corpse, then she gets the energy to kick him and drives him out. It indicates her husband is powerless to satisfy her sexual desire. She refuses to consider him as a human being. The usage of the weapon of the impotence of her husband by Champa works. It turns him into a useless creature in his own eyes. The simple biological fact of his impotency makes him alcoholic, weak, and wretched. He lost his entire self-dignity and surrenders to Champa. He says no, "I want her to beat me. Want to die at her hands. Don't want to live. Why live? No jobs, no wife, no home -- what's left (sobs loudly)—what is left?" (Act 3.Scene 3.190).This confession of Shinde proves his weakness and domination of Champa.

There is nothing great in one's being potent, or there is nothing shameful in one's being impotent. But it creates the conflict between impotent and potent, and it also reflects in powerless and powerful. If one accepts this simple biological fact without considering a social stigma, then only it can be transformed into a constructive force. Many times, social restrictions make a human being weak. It is important to note down here that impotency or potency both respectively make powerless and powerful.

Although the play is named after Sakharam Binder, it is Laxmi that assumes the lead in the end, as she emerges as the most important character in the play. Vasant Palshikar, a renowned critic, points out that the playwright may have thought of making Sakharam the protagonist of the play. "But the play slips from his hand; it becomes the play that focuses on the character of Laxmi, and it is she who becomes the real protagonist of the play" (Wadikar 9). The secret objective of Laxmi comes to the fore. Sakharam remains stupefied by watching the corpse of Champa as if "all the sap has been squeezed out of him" (Act 3.Scene 7.198). It is amazing to see how Laxmi gathers all her energy and digs a grave for Champato to save Sakharam from the law and live a life with him in the future. Sakharamthus loses all his power and egoism in the end.

Laxmi's reappearance from her distant and lone relations is not just because they have disowned her and falsely accused her of theft, but she returns as if to her own home. She had long before considered Sakhram's house as her own. She has everything and every instance connected with this place. It is probably her last hope, which initially provided a shelter. When she could not enkindle hope outside, she returned back with determination to change the condition of the house. Laxmi says, "I stayed here for a whole year. This house became my home. And now again" (Act 1.Scene 11.153).

The rude, as usual, Sakharam beats her and refuses to enter his house. He would not permit anyone to come in between himself and the fleshy Champa. But out of her feminine compassion, Champa helps her. She helps her also because of her practicality. These women are very much aware that they are helpless. Champa has an advantage of attractiveness, which gives her a slight edge over Laxmi's isolated state.

Both of these women share a similar fate in that both are expelled by their respective husbands, though the reasons may vary. We may not know much about Laxmi's past, but the playwright makes us aware of the experiences Champa has undergone while living with her husband. Champa, as we know, got married when she was just a minor, hardly aware of the meaning of marriage. She was married to a policeman who kept her in his house not as a human being but only as a female body to satisfy his lust. Sakharam is surprised to know that Champa used to beat her husband. Champa recalls the experiences of her painful life:

> No, I don't have a heart! He chewed it up raw long ago. [Pulls herself free.] He brought me from my mother even before I'd become a woman. He married me when I didn't even know what marriage meant...away. He brought me back and stuffed chilly powder into that god-awful place, where it hurts most. That bloody pimp! What's left of my heart now? (Act 2.Scene 2.167)

All these incidences reveal the conflict between powerful and powerless. The mutinous Champa doesn't allow herself to remain mute. Therefore, she breaks the silence and thus creates conflicts in Sakharam formulaic house. She straightforwardly rejects sexual advances by telling him that she was not that type of woman. It is only when he tries to make love again that she snatches the bottle from him and gulps the wine. She rebelliously declares that now she is ready to do all that he demands, even with a dog. In this way, or the other Champa cannot be qualified as a stereotyped ideal model of woman but a rebellious woman. Moreover, the striking difference between the two women shocks Sakharam as well as the audience. With the entry of Champa in the house, the rules of the house look to be getting shattered immediately. When Shinde comes, Sakharam takes a side of her husband. Though Sakharam condemns people's hypocrisy strongly, his words are very appropriate to his behaviour.

When we find the conflict within the relationships in the play, we can realize that by accepting all the rules of patriarchal society, Laxmi becomes weak and passive. Therefore, shehonestly performs all the domestic duties and is prepared to fulfill all the demands, including sexual demands of Sakharam. Being a champion of patriarchal values, he exploits her both physically and psychologically. Champa's physical appearance, on the other hand, captivates Sakharam, and gradually he surrenders and thus loses his power.

Sakharam opportunistically doesn't approve her calling her husband a corpse, pimp, an impotent lot, etc. Otherwise, he was the opponent of all husbands, surprisingly, and prevented her by asking her that she should not behave with him like that, as after all, he is her husband. After Sakharam witnesses Champa's wrath, it seems that he gets frightened and ready to change his earlier stance. His foundation is so shattered that he considers her as being possessed as she kicks, beats, and abuses her husband. The double standard and hypocrisy of male gender and fear of losing power are thus exposed.

The behavior and attitude of the main characters show their power, and it takes place in the conflicts. The theme of conflicts between powerful and powerless pervades throughout the play, and it explicitly reveals itself even in the minor characters. Laxmi's husband ruthlessly expels her simply because she could not bear children. She has not the courage to question him out of her traditional values and piety. She alone is responsible for their lack of children. She quietly surrenders to his irrational behavior and leaves the house. The helpless condition of Laxmi compels her to follow Sakharam.

Another character, Fouzdar Shinde, tortures Champa by beating her, sticking needles into her, and forcing her to do atrocious things. He frightens her away, brings her back again, and puts chili powder in her genitals. Owing to such degradable and horrible experience, she detests sex and so resists the physical advances of Sakharam later. Sakharam too finds sadistic pleasure in torturing Champa. He would get her drunk before her yields. He describes his wife's beauty so vulgarly that Sakharam feels contempt for him. In fact, all the characters in the play reveal the marks of good and evil, weakness and strength, and power and powerlessness.

By the end of the play, we see another fact, which is the female jealousy. Both Laxmi and Champa want to empower the soul of Sakharam in their own way. Women are largely responsible for their wretched condition. Champa shows sympathy to Laxmi and gives her shelter, but Laxmi turns cunningly. She assumes Champa is her rival in love and informs Sakharam about her illicit relationship with his friend Dawood. So, Laxmi is really a culprit of Champa's murder. Female jealousy finds in the play *Silence! The Court is in session,* where Mrs. Kashikar supports males to suppress Leela Benare.

Sakharam's beating of the people for being hypocrites and corrupt is indeed a matter of exploring. It might be the concept of ideal life, but still, the way he behaves equals him to the rest of the vulgar and degraded people. It is found that there are dreadful, discernible, and psychological differences in the nature of the protagonist and antagonist. Therefore, the conflict happens.

Sakharam loses all his power and becomes powerless in the end. All his selfishness and manly power vaporize in thin air. The man, whose egoism had never allowed others to rule over him, ironically loses all his freedom to a powerless and cast-off woman of his society. The comment of Chandrashekhar Barve is appropriate to judge Sakharam:

> Sakharam's ego tries to manifest itself in a challenging way. It is not ready to be tied down to anything. The influence of Laxmi triggers an inner conflict in Sakharam—the conflict between the existential ego

> and the metaphysical. In effect, we see that Sakharam, who has lost his self, has become pitiable because of his spinelessness, very much like a string without a kite. When he realizes that he is losing himself, he goes astray, he is frightened and finally, his living corpse gets pacified after lifeless and senseless activities. Sakharam is unpolished and the play Sakharam Binder appears to be rough. Nevertheless, the play does make its appearance with existentialist traits. (24)

The world portrayed in the play Sakharam Binder is obscene, physical, and evils of power and sex. The people in this world face conflict, and usually conflict occurs between powers and the powerless through their behavior, thoughts, and the rustic language they speak. It tends to destroy subtle sensibility and create distress and anguish. This world is not completely alien to the audience. It disturbs them, however, by shocking their moral consciousness.

Thus, the play deals with a bizarre conflict between powerful and powerless. This conflict appears in the life of Sakharam that destroys Champa's life. It also finds in Laxmi's life that awards her a permanent entry into Sakharm's house. He enjoys the social and masculine power in the form of a ruler of the house and the exploitation of women. The evils of power source give pain, suffering, and alienation not just for men but also for women in the play.

We can find a strange combination of power and privilege in contrast to pain and powerlessness not only in the life of Sakharam but also Champa and Laxmi. Everyone gets a chance to use power over others. Social and masculine power is being enjoyed by Sakharam in the forms of privilege that are seen in due course of the play. While Laxmi enjoys religious power and Champa uses her exceptional sensual beauty to privilege others. The fatal end of play dramatically manifests antithetical concerns while metaphorically pointing to the doom and decay of human beings, whose disillusioned lives let them not be the saviors but the survivors of humanity. The mental crisis has left them in conflict, chaos, concentration, and cowardice, eventually causing death-in-life and life-in-death due to an imbalance power that reflects in words, thoughts, deeds, and behavior.

We can easily see that the play is filled with conflicts and a lack of communication or interaction. Sometimes powerful becomes powerless and powerless and powerful in the conflicts because power always shifts from one to the other. In the beginning, Sakharam shows his mighty masculine power when he brings Laxmi into his home, and the same person begs Laxmi to save his life at the end. This kind of thread runs throughout the play.

Sakharam's worldly power obliges him to pay a huge cost for all other women, but he disregards the suffering and the varied indiscriminate forms of women. The end of play manifests contradictory affairs. It also metaphorically points out the downfall and deterioration of human beings.The psychological deadlock has left women in the maelstrom of conflict, clash, and fear that eventually causes a sense of inhumanity in words, thoughts, action, and behavior. By exposing the horrible environment in the contemporary social milieu, Tendulkar creates an explosion in the audiencemind and compels them to contemplate over it.

The title of the chapter is very significant, and the same conflict is associated with feminism. In this terminology, man is considered more powerful than woman, and she is regarded as powerless. Feminism tries to bring a balance between the two genders. We generally find that powerful people seem fortunate in that they seem able to do whatever they want. On the other hand, powerless people cannot do things because of a lack of power. As a consequence, when we hear or see the actions of the powerful, we judge them differently from those of the powerless; we may assume that the powerholder intended his or her action, but the powerless person is simply forced—bby circumstance or a stronger party—tto act. The same kind of picture is found in the play. The conflict finds not only in major characters like Sakharam, Laxmi, and Champa but also in minor characters like Dawood, Shinde, and Laxmi's husband. They all become victims of power and its effect. Shifting power from Sakharm to Champa and then again from Champa to Laxmi is an indication of the rights of individuals, and feminism advocates equality. So in this respect, Tendulkar is a feminist.

The world portrayed in the play Sakharam Binder is obscene, physical, evils of power and sex. The people in this world face the conflict and usually, conflict occurs between powers and powerless through their behavior, thoughts and the rustic language they speak. It tends to destroy subtle sensibility and creates distress and anguish. This world is not completely alien to the audience. It disturbs them, however, by shocking their moral consciousness.

Thus, the play deals with a bizarre conflict between powerful and powerless. This conflict appears in the life of Sakharam that destroys Champa's life. It also finds in Laxmi's life that awards her a permanent entry in Sakharm's house. He enjoys the social and masculine powerin the form of a ruler of the house and exploitation ofwomen. The evils of power source give pain, suffering, and alienation not just for men, but also for women in the play.

We can find a strange combination of power and privilege in contrast to pain and powerlessness not only in the life of Sakharam but also Champa and Laxmi. Everyone gets a chance to use power over others. Social and masculine power is being enjoyed by Sakharam in the forms of privilege that is seen in due course of the play. While Laxmi enjoys religious power and Champa uses her exceptional sensual beauty to privilege others. The fatal end of play dramatically manifests antithetical concerns while metaphorically pointing to doom and decay of human beings, whose disillusioned life letting them not to be the saviours but the survivors of humanity. The mental crisis has left them in the conflict, chaos, concentration, and cowardice, eventually causing death-in-life and life-in-death due to imbalance power that reflects in words, thoughts, deeds, and behaviour.

We can easily see that the play is filled with full of conflicts and lack of communication or interaction. Sometimes powerful becomes powerless and powerless and powerful in the conflicts because power always shifts from one to other. In the beginning, Sakharam shows his mighty masculine power when he brings Laxmi in his home and the same person begs to Laxmi to save his life at the end. This kind of thread runs throughout the play.

Sakharam's worldly power obliges him to pay a huge cost for all other women but he disregards the suffering and the varied indiscriminate forms of women. The end of play manifests contradictory affairs. It also metaphorically points out the downfall and deterioration of human beings.The psychological deadlock has left women in the maelstromof conflict, clash, and fear that eventually causes a sense of inhumanity in words, thoughts, action, and behaviour. By exposing the horrible environment in the contemporary social milieu, Tendulkar creates an explosion in theaudiencemind and compels them to contemplate over it.

The title of the chapter is very significant and the same conflict is associated with feminism. In this terminology, man is considered more powerful than woman and she is regarded as powerless. Feminism tries to bring a balance between the two genders. We generally find that powerful people seem fortunate is that they seem able to do whatever they want.On the other hand, powerless people cannot do because of lacking power.As a consequence, when we hear or see the actions of the powerful, we judge them differently from those of powerless; we may assume that the power holder intended his or her action, but the powerless person is simply forced — by circumstance or a stronger party — to act. The same kind of picture finds in the play. The conflict finds not only in major characters like Sakharam, Laxmi and Champa but also in minor characters like Dawood, Shinde and Laxmi's husband. They all become victims of power and its effect. Shifting power from Sakharm to Champa and then again from Champa to Laxmi is indication of rights of individuals and feminism advocates equality. So in this respect, Tendulkar is a feminist.

Works Cited

Agrawal, Beena. *Dramatic World of Vijay Tendulkar Exploration and Experimentations*. Jaipur: Aadi publications, 2012. Print.

Banerjee,Arundhati. "Introduction', *Five Plays, Vijay Tendulkar*. Bombay:OUP, 1992.Print.

Beauvoir, Simone de. *The Second Sex*. Trans. H. M. Parshley. New York: Alfred A Knoff, 1976.Print

Barve, Chandrashekhar. "Vijay Tendulkar: The Man Who Explores the Depths of Life." Studies in Contemporary Indian Drama. Ed. Sudhakar Pandey and Freya Taraporwala.New Delhi: Prestige, 1990. Print.

Dharan, N. S. *Salient Structural Features in Silence! And Kamala.*The Plays ofTendulkar. New Delhi: Creative Books, 1999.Print.

David G., Winter."A Psychological Reconstruction of the 20th Century and anIntellectual Agenda for Political Psychology."*Political Psychology* 21.2 (2000): 383-404. JSTOR.Web.28 Oct. 2010.Print.

Magde, V. M. Ed. *Vijay Tendulkar's Plays: An Anthology of Recent Criticism.*New Delhi: Pencraft Publication, 2009.Print.

Larsen,Neil.*The Discourse of Power: Culture Hegemony and the Authoritarian State.* Minneapolis: Institute for the Study of Ideologies and Literature,1983. Print.

Leeder,Elaine.The Family in Global Perspective: A GenderedJourney California: Sage, 2003. Print.

Limaye, Mohan R. "The Archetypal Identity of Laxmi in Sakharam Binder."*Modern Asian Studies,* Vol. 12, No. 1 (1978): 135-143. JSTOR.Web.20 July 2010.Print.

Mahesh Dattani and Mahasweta Devi.*Vijay Tendulkar's Plays: An Anthology of Recent Criticism.* Ed. V.M. Madge. New Delhi: Pencraft International, 2007. Print

Renuka, E.*All about Umbugland: A Study of Vijay Tendulkar's Plays.* Warangal:Diss.Kakatiya U,1984. Print.

Tendulkar, Vijay. *Five Play.* Sakharam Binder. Trans. Kumud Mehata andShanta Gokhale . New Delhi: OUP, 1974.pp.125-.198. Print.

Thankamma, Catherine. "Women that Patriarchy Created: The Plays of Vijay Tendulkar, Walters, and Margaret."*Feminism: A Very Short Introduction.* New York: Oxford U Press, 2005. Print.

Wadikar, Shailaja B.*Vijay Tendulkar A Pioneer Playwright.* New Delhi: Atlantic Publisher, 2008.Print.

----."Sakharam Binder: Tendulkar's Human Zoo." *The Criterion: An International Journal in English* 1.2 (2011): 1-12. Print.

7 Conclusion

Indian women are facing many issues like likedomestic violence, divorce, sexual harassment at work, rape, dowry, etc. in the present scenario. Though it is dark side, we can also see the great achievements are the reform in the field of law, which has given greater protection to women's rights. Women have been given support and protection through the right to property, the Domestic Violence Act 2005, reservations for women in different sectors, etc. Indian women have established their own stand by gaining high positions in all the fields, especially in the field of academics. They have also voiced with their various movements. We know very well how Indian women are trying to revive themselves. Women, who were earlier marginalized, are breaking the narrow boundaries. Women have been gaining freedom by linking themselves to all sections of people in society. Today, working women represent the nation. With the new phase of Indian history in which India has moved to global economy, we need the state to act strictly against any kind of crime against women so that women can have total equality at every level. Thus the vision of many Indian nationalists and that of playwrights like Vijay Tendulkar is getting fulfilled.

Vijay Tendulkar is a playwright and world figure. His plays are superb in characters, structure, and thematic richness. Tendulkar has played a giant role in putting the Indian theater on par with the world drama. His plays have offered an innovative and rich tradition to the Indian theater. His plays expose various aspects of our present society. Literature takes birth from the cultural ethos of that time and space. The natural harmony is always to be found between the literature of a particular time, space, and society of that time and space. Literature springs from culture and social circumstance; hence, all its aesthetics prove to be a social and cultural document of that particular time and space. The relation between literature and culture is an endless phenomenon. The writer's commitment is to bind the tuning between literature and the cultural ethos.

Tendulkar has secured an eminent place in the annals of Indian English drama with his experimental quest and exceptional vision. He becomes the torchbearer for the future generation of playwrights by breaking the established conventions. He establishes the fact that the drama is not just comprised of words but is a means of communication through performance. Along with the verbal, the non-verbal signs and symbols, too, are enacted as a gateway to the inner psyche of individual characters, and Tendulkar greatly succeeds in externalizing inner processes in his plays. His projection of social realism is not a mere copy of the stated reality, but rather it assumes a lively communication that reveals the inner conflict of the minds of his characters.

As a committed person, a committed writer observes the prevailing conditions and norms of his society in the real sense of the term, and so he can occupy the place in the reader's or audience's mind. If he lacks a sense of responsibility and commitment in his works, a writer would be futile. On the basis of the present research work on Vijay Tendulkar's plays, I assert that he is a great observer of society. If one tries to bring aesthetic sense to his writing, he may lose to conspiring at the prevailing realities of his time, culture, and society. Tendulkar is a great playwright who not only observes those stark realities but also exposes them faithfully through his plays.

Alienation of the modern individual, satirized contemporary politics, forcefully illustrated social and individual tension, portrayed the complexities of human character, and vigorously exploited man-woman relationships are an important issue that he discerns in his several literary works. Extensively, the themes that have most frequently paid his attention are the plight of a woman in a male-dominated urban middle-class society, the exploitation of women, and the husband-wife relationship as obtained in metropolitan centers like Bombay and Delhi. However, he frequently deals with major issues: gender, power, conflict, women's oppression, and violence.

After interpretation of Vijay Tendulkar's plays, it finds that Tendulkar is not a guru or philosopher. He is not one of those dramatists who uses the theme of drama in the service of his favorite socio-political ideology. He keeps aloof from any philosophy or ideology. He doesn't spread any particular philosophy of life. Some critics have pointed out a leftist interpretation to the plays like *Ghashiram Kotwal*, *Kamala,* and *Sakharam Binder*. It confirms that his plays are ready for diverse interpretations. Tendulkar cannot be tied down to a single line of thinking. We can say that his bent of mind is towards humanism, but it should also be wrong because his plays do not revolve in the orbit of that ideology either.

Most of Tendulkar's plays deal with the gyno-centric idea. He was essentially presenting the world, which rejected women's independence as citizens, enforced traditional Hindu-Brahmin norms of behavior, crushed her attempts at gaining freedom, and exercised rigid control over her sexuality and productivity. Tendulkar discovered two major tendencies of the patriarchal society, which are woman weakness and male dominance. Women were represented as suffering a lot at the hands of their male counterparts. They were exploited and marginalized in various ways.

He has dexterously infused feminine issues in his plays. His deeply felt agony for society is reflected throughout and indicates that his plays were not written with a commercial purpose; rather, they were the subjects that genuinely interested and captured his mind. He was all aware and a witness himself to a number of ills prevalent in society. Therefore, his themes come directly from lived, felt, and experienced reality. In other words, his plays are a kind of mirror reflecting social reality in a completely detached and objective manner. They are indeed the means to show his unmatched vision, genuine reactions, and earnest feelings for the existent panorama.

His plays are faithful records and exposures of what he has seen and observed in close quarters of life. His early journalistic background aided him to see things and see them in their entirety. Therefore, it aided, in turn, to transform the socio-political situation into an explosive drama. He forcefully and naturally depicted modern-day social and individual alienation. The contemporary politics is satirized with superb skill along with the revelation of the complexities of human character. His understanding of the man-woman relationship is superb and found exclusive expression in many of his plays. Most notably, his plays deal with the predicament of women in a male-dominated society. In his plays, we have mostly the urban middle-class society and the husband-wife relationship as extracted from metropolitan cities like Bombay and Delhi. Undoubtedly, his plays touch every aspect of human life, but he seems to underline the major issues like violence, gender, and power politics.

Although feminism as a movement and feminism as a theory and concern in Indian literature has entered as a by-product of western feminist movement, one can observe and estimate the contribution of Indian freedom struggle, spared of education, and the provisions in the Indian constitution that greatly brought awareness in regard to rights among women. Today, women in India are greatly conscious and alert about their rights and can raise their voice against the exploitation of any kind. The writers are generally sensitive to the happenings around in general and the exploitation of women in particular. Many Indian women novelists like Anita Desai, Kamala Markandaya, Ruth Prawer Jhabvala, Nayantara Sahgal, Shashi Deshpande, Shobha De, Githa Hariharan, Namita Gokhale Manju Kapur, Mahasweta Devi, and Githa Hariharan, to name a few, have explored female subjectivity in their fiction. But the genre drama somehow lagged behind in exposing the degradation and exploitation of women in Indian society, and with Tendulkar, the issues of women are authentically found in their expression and serious contemplation. Moreover, he was criticized too on account of the truthful presentation of the predicament of a woman in a male-dominated society. His contention was that he has not cheated his generation nor attempted to simplify the matters for his audience, but what he has presented was seen and perceived by him.

The analysis undertaken in the previous chapters is quite sufficient to put forth final findings and can reveal the voice of Tendulkar is in favor of feminism. His plays unravel his advanced perceptions, which faithfully indicate his revolt against the traditional setup of patriarchy and that he has asserted his stout belief in the empowerment of women. The playwright may have denied being a feminist as such, but the consciousness about women's issues in his plays is not only perceptible but obvious. For, one may easily observe that the central figure of his plays is mostly a woman, and that woman is a significant character who plays the role of a protagonist. The reverberation of feminist elements is clearly perceptible in his plays, and the plays represent his progressive ideas. The carefully written dialogues in the plays faithfully render and replicate the status of women in the family and social life. The issues such as discrimination on the basis of sex, the dominance of patriarchy, and gender bias have been so naturally and efficiently exposed in the plays under deepth.

The present book dealt with the concept of feminism – feminism in India—The Dramatic World of Vijay Tendulkar—Tendulkar as a feminist. The mind and art of the playwright reveal his leanings to social activism that necessarily turned him into the advocate of the neglected unit of society, i.e., women. He assumes the role of a courageous commentator on society.

Tendulkar exposes women characters in different visions beyond the reformative zeal of the defender of feminist ideology. The character Leela Benare in **Silence** is an intellectual woman. She retains her femininity and her inner strength to challenge the force of patriarchal exploitation, while Laxmi and Champa in Sakharam Binder represent two opposites' images of womanhood. Both are victims of a male-dominated world, but they retain their spark of individuality and register their protest. The playwright unfolds Laxmi in spite of a weak, poor, and kind-hearted woman who declares her freedom in the form of leaving Sakhram‘s house even though she has no shelter. The representation of Champs's authority subdues Sakharm‘s masculinity. Both women are revolutionary in patriarchal culture. They revolt against the male dominance culture. It clearly reveals that Tendulkar‘s artistic and dramatist sense bends towards feminism.

Kamala exposes the double standard of male ego, the oppression, and exploitation of women, but at the same time, it reflects female liberation and attributes strong will for freedom amidst egocentric patriarchal dominance. Vijay Tendulkar deals with other social issues, too; this play is sensitive and accurate, and it is prominently gyno-centric in the sense.

The play is built on the transformation of Sarita, who emerges from an obedient wife to an assertive and rebellious woman for her identity. Hefaithfully rendered the male-dominated world having positivity or an optimistic perspective that women can emerge as courageous and capable of liberating themselves by challenging the male chauvinists in society.

Woman and nature both have the property of reproduction as well as love and compassion. Therefore, it necessitates every individual to safeguard her from oppression and exploitation. On the contrary, man exploits equally both nature and woman for his benefits and loses its dignity and divinity. Vijay Tendulkar condemns the very attitude that attributes secondary status to a woman. It is an admitted fact that even today men beat, suppress, and even kill women to satisfy their male ego. They enjoy the role of exploiter, least caring for the inevitable outcome. The sense of superiority on the part of males creates many problems like child marriage, sexual harassment, the disparity in education, domestic violence, dowry and female infanticide, etc. Women face violence within the family (dowry-related harassment, death, marital rape, wife-battering, sexual abuse, deprivation of healthy food, female genital mutilation, etc.) or outside the family (kidnapping, rape, murder, etc.).

The surrounding atmosphere must be taken into consideration when Tendulkar began writing. The surrounding atmosphere and contemporary scenario were filled with bleak aspects like murders, crimes, rape, loss of moral values, extramarital affairs, political injustice, the lust of power, greed of money, and so on, but very few authors of the time had courage enough or attempted to write upon it. Tendulkar, on the other hand, smashes the rule of customary and habitual writings and uses his writing skills for the awakening of his readers. He observes the plight, exploitation, and degradation of women in contemporary society. He gave voice to these follies in his plays and gave a new dimension to the Indian drama through his dramatic art.

Broadly speaking, the artistic appeal is an important part of any literary work. It decides the success or failure of the work of art. A work of art with an everlasting appeal always remains eternal. It will not be an overstatement that the same thing eternal appeal is attributed to Tendulkar's plays, for even today we notice, read, and hear about the victims like Kamala, Benare, and Sarita. Similarly, we see males like Sakharam, Jaisingh Jadav, Ghashiram, etc. around us in society. Their socio-economic background may differ, but they have one thing in common: males consider women inferior, something to be exploited or as their sole possessions. The appeal of his plays will be unending so long as such characters find themselves in society as a living reality. Thus, his plays bear relevancy during our times. The plays are a faithful demonstration and powerful commentary on the social, political, and cultural life of man in modern times. They are powerful manuscripts on the mess of women and feminism

The conflict between powerful and powerless is faithfully finding in Sakharam *Binder*. The playwright adopts a character-centric approach and highlights the exploitation of women at the hands of the exploiter, hedonist, and an egoist Sakharam. Power is the dominant factor that reflects in the play and arouses the conflict on various issues. He utilizes his power to exploit and suppress the women in his life. He cherishes and wants to set out a strange morality of his own by revolting against marriage institutions. The egoist cares for his own survival and dominance, though he himself is being outcast. Ironically, he exploits the more helpless, the cast-off women.

By exposing the desire, the ache for life, and the lower stratum of society, the playwright made a significant exit from the prevailing typical of Marathi drama. Tendulkar has for the first time introduced the life and characters of lower strata with all shades of its ugliness and vulgarity, which has been burning, shocking,, and unbearable for those who are habitual to seeing the lives of a privileged section of society. *Sakharam Binde*r a fine illustration of the mentioned situation.

The women in the play, Laxmi and Champa, are projected as victims, and by rendering a faithful portrayal of them, the playwright exposes the existence—individual and social—of harmony and disharmony. Tendulkar explores complications of human relations and nature by bringing out the dramatic tension among Laxmi, Champa, and Sakharam. This play, as it may be surmised from the present study, is a study of violence in human beings, the oppression and seduction, and the depth of physical lust. It presents the ugliness and crudity of male desire to dominate and exploit women. In short, the ideas and views expressed in the play are thought-provoking and revolutionary. Undoubtedly, the playwright surprises the conventional audience by rejecting the established norms and conventional morality.

In Sakharam, we see an inner urge to change some of the social conditions around him, and as he fails in bringing about the change owing to personal limitations, he vents his anger and frustration on the powerless women in his life. So it raises conflict between Laxmi and Sakharm, Champa and Sakharam. He exerts his manly power and dominance over women who seem to be powerless in a given society, but the playwright shows how the power can be transferable. It is an undeniable fact that Indian society greatly nourishes and encourages inequalities and therefore remains split between the haves and have nots—the power.

The play further represents two worlds. One is the public morality world, an existing family or institution of a marriage governed by caste, religion, traditions, and morality; another is the anti-family or private morality world created by Sakharam. Tendulkar gives very complex minute details of experiences of gender violence in the married lives of these two diametrically opposite sets of women, Laxmi and Champa.

The analysis of Vijay Tendulkar's plays concludes that his feminist approach discovers the same in most of his plays. Without allowing interference, he puts forth burning issues of contemporary society and times. He presents his characters on the stage as free individuals. They live according to their inner desire and inner landscape, so they give the touch of reality to his plays. Nowhere his characters appear as puppets in his hands. They live, love, and suffer because of their own way of life. They are round and dynamic in nature, whether they remain for a short or long span of time before the audience. Tendulkar believed that the playwright needs to be an actor-writer who plays 'roles' as he writes, and it helped Tendulkar in depicting the characters as he was associated with the theater. According to him, characterization in a play is to a large extent revealed through the dialogue. Therefore, the playwright must have a moldable and not a rigid style of writing. He must change his style with every character, and Tendulkar as a playwright followed this.

Only a few plays of his prolonged literary career are available in good English translation; therefore, any critical work of a researcher not familiar with the Marathi language is not able to access the whole of his composition. The present research focused only on a few important and selected dramatic works of Vijay Tendulkar.

Tendulkar's woman character ought to be subjugated or suppressed in the course of the play, but they have courage to retain their claim of individuality and womanhood. Their violence against male dominancemight be against the principles of femininity but they construct the wave of resistance in which the parable of social principles becomes feeble and insignificant.

Vijay Tendulkar, with his dramatic spirit, expanded the horizons of Indian theater. His realistic representation of social problems has been the subject of serious discourse in postcolonial India. To make drama more effective and relevant, Tendulkar understood and came down to the consciousness of the audience and made the synthesis of the relative of society with the art of theater.

The plays reveal that Vijay Tendulkar is a staunch supporter of feminism. So he is a feminist playwright. His plays introduce us to the pathetic condition of the very sensible. By observing his plays keenly, it may be summed up that he is a feminist, and feminism is the essence of his writings.

Bibliography

Primary Sources

Tendulkar, Vijay. *Five Play*. Silence! The Court is in Session. Trans. Priya Adarkar. New Delhi: OUP, 1974.pp. 55-121. Print.

—Kamala. *Five Plays*. Trans. Priya Adarkar. New Delhi: Oxford University, Press, 1995.pp.1-52. Print.

—*Five Play*. Sakharam Binder. Trans.Kumud Mehata and Shanta Gokhale. New Delhi: OUP, 1974.pp.125-.198. Print.

Secondary Sources

Abboston, Susan C. W. *Thematic Guide to Modem Drama*. London: Greenwood Press, 2003. Print.

Abrams, M. H., and Geoffery Gait Harpham.*A Handbook of Literary Terms*.New Delhi: Cengage Learning, 2009. Print.

Agrawal, Beena. *Dramatic World of Vijay Tendulkar: Explorations and Experimentations*. Jaipur: Aadi Publications, 2003. Print.

Althusser, Louis. "Ideology and Ideological State Apparatuses: Notes towards an Investigation." *Lenin and Philosophy Other Essays*.Trans. Bren Brewster.New York: Monthly Review Press, 1971. Print.

—. and E. Bailber. *Reading Capital*. London: New Left Books, 1970. Print.

Bandyopadhyay, Samik. *Vijay Tendulkar :Collected Plays in Translation*. New Delhi: Oxford U Press, 2003. Print.

Barat, Urvashi, *When Writing is Life Itself*. New Delhi: Asia Book Club, 2002 Print.

Barve, Chandrashekhar. "Vijay Tendulkar: The Man Who Explores the Depths of Life." *Studies in Contemporary Indian Drama.*Ed. Sudhakar Pandey andFreya Taraporwala.New Delhi: Prestige, 1990. Print.

Barbuddhe, S. andAmar Nath Prasad (ed). *The Plays of Vijay Tendulkar: Critical Explorations.* New Delhi: Sarup and Sons, 2008.Print.

Barry, Peter. *Beginning Theory: An Introduction to Literary and Cultural Theory.* Ed. Manchester: Manchester U Press, 2007. Print.

Beauvoir, Simone de.*The Second Sex.* Trans. H. M. Parshley. New York: Alfred A Knoff, 1976. Print.

Bhagat, R. M..(ed.). Political Thought: Plato to Marx, 1961. 12 Jalandhar: New Academic Publishing Co., 2009. Print.

Banerjee, Arundhati, "Introduction", *Five Plays of Vijay Tendulkar.* Bombay: OUP, 1992: iii Print.

---. Appendix I. "Note on Kamala, Silence! The Court is in Session, Sakharam Binder, The Vultures, Encounter in Umbugland". *Collected Plays in Translation* .NewDelhi:OUP. 2003. Print.

Black, Max(ed.).*Social Theories of Talcott Parsons: A Critical Examination.* Endwood Cliffs N. J.: Prentice-Hall Inc., 1961. Print.

Butler, Christopher. *Postmodernism: A Very Short Introduction.* New York: Oxford U. Press, 2002. Print.

Butler, Judith. *Gender Trouble.* New York: Routledge, 1990. Print.

Champaklal, Mahesh.*Depiction of Sex and Violence in Vijay Tendulkar's Play inthe Context of The Prevailing Social Economical andPolitical Conditions ofIndia.*Diss.U Baroda.Privately Published2013.Print.

Chancer, Lynn S. and Beverly Xaviera Watkins.*Gender, Race and Class: An Overview.* Blackwell Publishing India, 2007. Print.

Chitnis, Suma. *Alphabet of Lust.* Kenyan Review, Vol. VIII. 1951. Print.

Chopra, Dr. Ravi. *Advanced Essays.* New Delhi: Bookhive, 1980.Print.

Carden, Maren Lockwood. *The New Feminist Movement.* Russel Sage Foundation, 1974. Print.

Clare O'Farrell. *Michel Foucault.* London: Sage Publications, 2005. Print.

Crampton, Jeremy and Stuart Elden (eds). *Space, Knowledge and Power.* Hampshire: Ashgate, 2007. Print.

Dasgupta, Sanjukta and Malashri Lai(eds).*The Indian Family in Transition: Reading Literary and Cultural Texts.*Los Angeles: Sage Publications, 2007. Print.

Dass, Veena Noble. *Modern Indian Drama in English Translation*, New Delhi: Creative, 1999.Print

De Beauvoir, Simone. *The Second Sex.* Harmondsworth: Penguin, 1952. Print.

Dharan, N.S. *The Plays of Vijay Tendukkar.* New Delhi: Creative Books, 1999.Print.

—. *Theatres of Independence: Drama, Theory, and Urban Performance in India since1947.* New Delhi: Oxford U. Press, 2008. Print.

Durant, Will. The Story of Philosophy. New York: Pocket books, 2006. Print

---.*The Story of Civilization* Part I .New York: Simon & Schuster, 1963. Print.

Eagleton,Mary(ed). *A Concise Companion to FeministTheory.* Oxford: Blackwell, 2003 Print.

Esslin, Martin. *Theatre of the Absurd* .Lodon: Penguin, 1968.Print.

Eagleton, Terry. *Ideology: An Introduction.* London: Verso, 1991. Print.

EmberCarol R. and Melvin Ember (eds.) *Encyclopedia of Sex and Gender: Men and Women in the World's Cultures.* New York: Kluwer Academic and Plenum Publishers, 2003. Print.

Freud, Sigmund.*New Introductory Lectures on Psychoanalysis*, New York: Penguin, 1977.Print.

Gamble,Sarah (ed). *The Routledge Companion to Feminism and Postfeminism.* London and New York: Routledge, 2001. Print.

---.*The Routledge Companion to Feminism and Post-feminism*.London: Routledge, 2006. Print.

Gangoli, Geetanjali. *Indian Feminisms: Law, Patriarchies and Violence in India*. Hampshire: Ashgate Publishing Limited, 2007. Print.

Geuss, Raymond. *The Idea of a Critical Theory: Habermas and the Frankfurt School.* London: Cambridge U. Press, 1981. Print.

Gokhle, Shanta. *Vijay Tendulkar*. New Delhi: Katha, 2001. Print.

Grimke, Sarah. *Letters on the Equality of the Sexes and the Condition of Woman*.New York: Burt Franklin, 1970.Print.

Guha. Ed. J.P .(ed).*History of the Maharattas*.Vol. 2.New Delhi: Associated Publishing,1978.Print.

Heywood, Andrew, *Political Ideologies*, Pal grave Macmillan, 2003, Print.

Harris, Maria. "Silence."*Encyclopaedia of Feminist Feminist Literary Theory*.Ed.Elizabeth Kowaleski Wallace. London: Routledge, 2009. Print.

Hutcheon, Linda. *Postmodernism and Feminism: Canadian Context*. Ed. ShirinKudechedkar. New Delhi: Pencraft International, 1995.Print.

lyenger, K R Srinivasa. *Indian Writing in English*.Sterling Publishers,n.d. Print.

Iyer, N. Sharda. *Musings on Indian Writing in English*.Vol. 3.New Delhi: Samp and Sons, 2007. Print.

Jack, Dana C. and Alisha Ali. *Silencing the Self across Cultures Depression and Gender In the Social World.* New York: Oxford U Press, 2010. Print.

Jardine, Alice. *Gynesis: Configurations of Women and Modernity*. Ithaca: Cornell U.P, 1986. Print.

Jain Jasbir,*Indigenous Roots of Feminism*. New Delhi: Sage Publications, 2011.Print.

---and Singh, Avadhesh Kumar. *Indian Feminisms*. New Delhi: Creative Books,2001Jones, Steve. *Antonio Gramasci*. London: Routeldge, 2006. Print.

Joseph, Sarah. *Political Theory and Power*. Delhi: Foundation Books, 2004. Print.

Kanwar, Asha S. *Ghashiram Kotwal: A Study Guide*. New Delhi: IGNOU, 1993. Print.

Kapoor, Kapil. "Hindu Women, Traditions and Modernity".in*Feminism, Tradition and Modernity*. Ed. Chandrakala Padia. New Delhi: Glorious Printers, 2002.

Kapadia, K. M. *Marriage and Family in India*. 1966. Calcutta: Oxford U. Press, 1994. Print.

Kaufmann, Walter(ed).*The Will to Power*. New York: Vintage Books, 1968. Print.

Ketkar, Kumar. "Tendulkar's Human Zoo",*The illustrated weekly*, 20Nov., 1983, 22.Print.

Kellner, Douglas M. and Meenakshi Gigi Durham (eds.). *Media and Cultural Studies: Key Works*. Maiden: Blackwell Publishing, 2006. Print.

Klein, M. *Our Adult World and its Roots in Infancy*.London .1960.Quoted in *The Psychology of Tragic Drama* (ed.) Patrick Roberts.Routledge and Kegan Paul, 1975.Print.

King,Kimball(ed.). *Western Drama Through the Ages*. Vol. 1. London: Greenwood Press, 2007. Print.

Krolokkle, Charlotte and Anne Scott Soreson.*Gender Communication: Theories and Analysis. From Silence to Performance*. California: Sage Publication, 2006. Print.

Kuthari, Asha. *Mahesh Dattani: An Introduction*. Delhi: Foundation Books, 2005. Print.

Larsen,Neil.*The Discourse of Power: Culture Hegemony and the Authoritarian State*. Minneapolis: Institute for the Study of Ideologies and Literature, 1983. Print.

Leeder, Elaine.*The Family in Global Perspective: A GenderedJourney* California: Sage, 2003. Print.

Leitch, Vincent B.(ed).*The Norton Anthology of Theory and Criticism.*New York: Norton, 2001. Print.

---(ed.). *The Ego and Its Own.*Cambridge: Cambridge U. press, 1995. Print.

Lai, Malashri. *Women Writers in Indian English.* Simla: Indian Institute of Advanced Study, 1995. Print.

Luktuke, Ulhas."Abhar!Rangachya Ewadhya Tukadyasathi",*Kesari,* Translated by Shailaja Wadekar Mar.29, 1970. Print

Madge, V.M.(ed.). *Vijay Tendulkar's Plays: An Anthology of Recent Criticism.* Ed. Delhi: Pencraft International, 2007. 130-143. Print.

Macey, David.*Dictionary of Critical Theory.* London: Penguin, 2000. Print.

Mahesh Dattani and Mahasweta Devi.*Vijay Tendulkar's Plays: An Anthology of Recent Criticism.* Ed. V.M. Madge. New Delhi: Pencraft International, 2007. Print

Marx, Carl and Friedrich Engels.*Manifesto of the Communist Party.* Utrecht: Open Source Socialist Publishing, 2008. Print.

McHoul, Alec and Wendy Grace. *A Foucault Primer: Discourse, Power and the Subject.* London: Routledge, 2002. Print.

Mills, Sarah. Michel Foucault. London: Routledge, 2007. Print.

Mishra,Kamal K.and Janet Huber Lowxy(eds). *Recent Studies on Indian Women.* Jaipur: Rawat Publications, 2007. Print.

Mulye Pradip, Rajiv Naik & Vijay Tapas(eds.). *Ten Ani Amhi.*Awishkar Prakashan, Mumbai, 1992.Print.

Naikar, Basavaraj. *Literary Vision.* New Delhi: Sarup and Sons, 2005. Print.

Naipaul,V.S. "Foreword". *India: A Wounded Civilization.* London: Picador, 2001. Print.

Nayantara, Uma. *Indian Women writer's at the Cross Roads.* New Delhi: Pen crafts, 1996. Print.

Nehru, Jawaharlal. *The Discovery of India.*Centenary edition. Delhi: Oxford U.P, 1989. Print.

Offen, Karen. "Defining Feminism: a comparative historical approach" *Beyond Equality and Difference: Citizenship, Feminist Politics, and Female Subjectivity.* Eds. Gisela Bock and Susan James. London: Routledge, 1999. Print.

Omvedt, Gail. *We shall Smash This Prison: Indian Woman Struggle.* London: Zed Books, 1980.Print.

Padia, Chandrakala. "Feminism, Tradition and Modernity: An Essay in Relation toManusmriti'.*Feminism, Tradition and Modernity.* Ed.Chandrakala Padia. New Delhi: GloriousPrinters2002.

Pandey, Sudhakar and Freya Taraporwala (eds.). *Studies in Contemporary Indian Drama.* New Delhi: Prestige, 1990. Print.

Pandey, Sudhakar and FreyaBarwa(eds.). *Directions in Indian Drama.*New Delhi: Prestige Books, 1994. Print.

Parsons, Talcott. "Authority, Legitimation and Political Action.'"*Authority.*Ed. Carl J. Friedrich. Cambridge: Harvard U Press, 1958. 197-221. Print.

Panigrahi, Ramesh P. "The Distribution of Power in American Society." *World Politics*10 (1957): 123-43. Print.

Payne, Michael and Jessica Rae Barbera (eds.). *A Dictionary of Cultural And Critical Theory.* West Wessex: Wiley-Blackwell, 2010. Print.

Peter Collier(ed.). *European Connections*(Vol. 19). Ed.. Oxford: Peter Lang, 2006. Print.

Peer, Basharat.*Curfewed Night.* New Delhi: Random House, 2008. Print.

Plato. *Republic.*Trans. Desmond Lee. New York: Penguin Books, 1974. Print.

Poulantzas, Nicos. *Political Power and Social Class.* London: New Left Books, and Sheed Ward, 1978. Print.

Prasad, Amar Nath and Satish Barbuddhe.(eds.).*The Plays of Vijay Tendulkar: Critical Explorations.*New Delhi: Sarup and Sons, 2008. Print.

Protevi, John (ed).*The Edinburgh Dictionary of Continental Philosophy*. Edinburgh: Edinburgh U Press, 2005. Print.

Paul, Smita. *Theatre of Power*.Books Way Publishers & Distributors. Kolkata 2010. Print.

Radhai, K. *Treatment of Reality, Fantasy and Myth in the Select Plays of Girish Karnad.* Bharathiar U: Diss. Erode Arts College,, Erode. 2006. Print.

Rafia, M. H. Mohammed. "Women in Vijay Tendulkar's *Kamala*".*The Quest*.Vol.17.No2. 2.Decemeber, (2003): 63-65. Print.

Rahman, L. (2010). "Tendulkar's 'Silence! The Court is in Session": *A Study in Perspectives.* Kolkata: Books Way Publishers & Distributors.2010.Print.

Renuka, E.*All about Umbugland: A Study of Vijay Tendulkar's Plays.* Warangal: Diss. Kakatiya U, 1984. Print.

Rothschild, K. W. *Power in Economics.* Harmondsworth: Penguin, 1971. Print.

Sathe,Makarand..*Vijay Tendulkar: Omnibus.* Delhi: Arvind Kumar Publishers, 2007. Print.

Sujatha K.R., and Gokilavani, S. *Feminine Aesthetics of Indian Women Writers.* New Delhi: Regal Publications, 2011. Print.

---."Tendulkar and violence – Then and Now" in a documentary *Interview of Vijay Tendulkar.*

Thankamma, Catherine. "Women that Patriarchy Created: The Plays of Vijay Tendulkar, Mahesh Dattani and Mahasweta Devi." *Vijay Tendulkar's Plays: An Anthology of Recent Criticism.* Ed.V.M. Madge. New Delhi: Pencraft International, 2007. Print.

Saran, Satya, and Vimal Patil."An Interview with Vijay Tendulkar, *Femina.*(June 8-22), 1984.37. Print.

Smart, Barry. Ed. *Michel Foucault.* New York: Routledge, 1985.Print.

Schmitt, Richard. *Introduction to Marx and Engels: A Critical Reconstruction.* 2nded. Oxford: WesternPress, 1997. Print.

Shakespeare, William. *Hamlet.* New York: Bantom Books, 1980. Print.

Sharma, Arvind. "How to Read the Manusmriti".in*Feminism, Tradition and Modernity.* Ed. Chandrakala Padia. New Delhi: Glorious Printers, 2002.

Simon, Shibu. Man-Woman Relationship in the Plays of Vijay Tendulkar.*The Plays of Vijay Tendulkar Critical Explorations.*eds. Amar Nath Prasad, Satish Barbuddhe. New Delhi:Sarup & Sons, 2008. Print.

Smith, Nicholas D. "Plato and Aristotle on the Nature of Women".*Journal of the History of Philosophy.* **21** *(4)(1983): 467–478.*

Singh, Avadhesh Kumar. "Self or Motherhood: Is that the Question?". in*Indian Feminisms* Eds. Jasbir Jain, Avadhesh Kumar Singh. New Delhi: CreativeBooks, 2001.Print.

Sircar ,Badal. *Two Plays.*New Delhi: Oxford U Press, 2010. Print.

Srinavas, M. N. *Social Change in Modern India.* New Delhi: Orient Blackman, 1966. Print.

Sujatha K.R., and Gokilavani, S. *Feminine Aesthetics of Indian Women Writers.* New Delhi: Regal Publications, 2011.Print.

Tendulkar, Vijay. *Collected Plays in Translation.* Trans. Jayant Karve and Eleanor Gokhle. New Delhi: Oxford U Press, 2003. Print.

Tiwari, Subha. "Silence! The Court is in Session: A strong Social Commentary"*Contemporary of Indian Dramatists.* Ed. Shubha Tiwari. New Delhi: Atlantic Publisher, 2007.Print.

Wadikar, Shailaja B.*Vijay Tendulkar A Pioneer Playwright.* New Delhi: Atlantic Publisher, 2008.Print.

---."Sakharam Binder: Tendulkar's Human Zoo."*The Criterion: A InternationalJournal in English* 1.2 (2011): 1-12. Print.

Wallace,Elizabeth Kowaleski (ed). *Encyclopedia of Feminist Literary Theory.* London: Routledge, 2009. Print.

Walters, Margaret. *Feminism: A Very Short Introduction.* New York: Oxford U Press,2005. Print.

West, Rebecca. *The Young Rebecca: Writing of Rebecca West* -1911-1917. ed. Jane Marcus London: Macmillan, 1982. Print.

Wyckoff, Hogie. "Sex role scripting in men and women," *Scripts People Live*. Ed. Claude M. Steiner, New York: Bantam, 1980

Webliography

Amossy, Ruth."Introduction to the Study of Doxa."*Poetics Today* 23 (2002): 369-394. Project Muse.Web.Retrived.26 Aug.2016.<iteseerx.ist.psu.edu/viewdoc/download?doi=10.1.1.825.7308&rep=rep1&type=pdf>

Asthana, Shaily."Vijay Tendulkar's Theatre of Violence, Defiance and Confidence."Litsearch 2.3 (August, 2012): 18-23. Litsearch.in. Web. Retrived.19Sep.2016.<https://shodhganga.inflibnet.ac.in/bitstream/10603/110706/7/11_chapter2.pdf>

Bates, Thomas R. "Gramsci and the Theory of Hegemony."*Journal of the History of Ideas* 36.2 (1975): 351-366. JSTOR.Web.Retrived. 10 Aug. 2017.<https://www.academia.edu/9855907/>

Bhaneja, Balwant. "Vijay Tendulkar (1928-2008)." HotReview.org. Hunter Department of Theater, n.d. Web.Retrived .30 June 2016.

< http://www.hotreview.org/articles/vijaytendulkar.htm>

Cixous, Helene, Keith Cohen, Paoula Cohen. "The Laugh of Medusa." Signs 1.4 (1976):875- 893. JSTOR.Web.Retrived. 22 Apr. 2006.

<https://shodhganga.inflibnet.ac.in/>

David G., Winter."A Psychological Reconstruction of the 20th Century and an Intellectual Agenda for Political Psychology."*Political Psychology* 21.2 (2000): 383-404.JSTOR.Web.Retrived.28 Oct. 2016.

<https://academictree.org/psych/publications.php?pid=25978>

Desai, Hemang. "Polarity in Female Psyche: Burrowing in the Mystery in Silence the Court is in Session." AuthorsDen.com. 20 Sep. 2008. Web.Retrived.9 Mar. 2017.<https://shodhganga.inflibnet.ac.in>

Deshpande, G.P."Marathi Literature since Independence: Some Pleasures and Displeasures." *Economicand Political Weekly* 32.44(Nov. 8-15): 2885-2892.J570i?.Web.Retrived. 20 July 2016.<ttps://studyres.com/doc/>

Dharwadker, Apama Bhargava. "India's Theatrical Modernity: Re-Theorizing Colonial, Postcolonial, and Diasporic Formations." *Theatre Journal* 63 (2011)425-437. JSTOR.Web.Retrived. 15 Nov. 2018.<https://studyres.com/doc/14989116/chap>

Goldman, Robert P. "Trans-sexualism, Gender, and Anxiety in Traditional India."*Journal of the American Oriental Society* 113.3 (1993): 374-401. JSTOR.Web.Retrived.19 May 2015

< https://shodhganga.inflibnet.ac.in/bitstream>.

Joseph, S. John Peter. "The playwright as Social Critic: A Critical Study ofVijay Tendulkar's Silence! The Court is in Session." *The Journal for English Language and LiteraryStudies*.n.d. Web. Retrived .9 Mar. 2016.<www.tjells.com/article/27_JOHN PETER JOSEPH.pdf>

Panigrahi, Ramesh P. "On the Concept of Political Power." *Proceedings of the American Philosophical Society 1*07.3 (1963): 232-262. JSTOR. Web.Retrived 13 Dec. 2015.<https://shodhganga.inflibnet.ac.in/bitstream/10603/63174/12/12_conclusion.pdf>

Pandey, Pramila. "Vijay Tendulkar's Play Kamala: A Symbol of Slavery."*Journal of Teaching and Research in English Literature* 3.2 (2011): N.p.Web.Retrived.12May2017.https://shodhganga.inflibnet.ac.in/bitstream/10603/63174/12/12/- conclusion.pdf

Pierrot, Anne Harschberg. "Barthes and Doxa."*Poetics today* 23 (2002): 427- 442.Project Muse. Web. Retrived.13 Dec. 2016

<https://shodhganga.inflibnet.ac.in/bitstream/10603/63174/7/07_chapter %202.pdf>

Shah, Mihir. "Structures of Power in Indian Society: A Response." *Economic and Political Weekly* (15 Nov. 2008) 78-83. Samprag.org. Web. Retrived.20Nov.2015.https://www.epw.in/journal/2008/46/discussion /structures-power-indian-society-response.html

Rai, Deepak Kumar."Tradition versus Modernity in the Indian Marriage Custom in Mahesh Dattani's Do the Needful." *International Journal of Humanities and Social Sciences Invention III.III (2014): 11-17. Web. Retrived. 10 December 2015.<http://www.ijhssi.org>.*

Winter, David G. "A Psychological Reconstruction of the 20th Century and an Intellectual Agenda for Political Psychology."*Political Psychology.*.21.2 (2000):383-404JSTOR.Web.2Oct.2016.<ttps://www.researchgate.net/scientific-contributions/58389943_David_G_Winter>

Adhikari, Ramesh"Portrayal of 'New Woman' with Special Reference toHenrik Ibsen's The Doll's House and Vijay Tendulkar's Kamala. Web.Retrived.accessed on 18 oct.2017<https://www. pingpdf.com/pdf-depiction-of-sex-and-violence-in-vijay-to-parent->

Champaklal, Mahesh. *Depiction of Sex and Violence in Vijay Tendulkar'sPlay inthe Context of The Prevailing Social Economical andPolitical Conditions ofIndia.* Diss.U Baroda.Privately Published 2013.Web.Retrived. 12 December 2015<https://pingpdf.com/pdf-depiction-of-sex-and-violence-invijay-to-parent-directory.html>

Kundu,Tanmoy." Exploitation of Women in Vijay Tendulkar's PlaysSilence!TheCourt is in Sessionand Kamala"*Galaxy: InternationalMultidisciplinaryResearchjournal*Web.Retrived. 12 December 2015https://docplayer.net/33320469-Exploitation-of-women-invijay-tendulkar-s-plays-silence-the-court-is-in.html

UC Press E-Books Collection, 1982-2004. 2004. University of California Libraries. Web. 15 May 2014. <http://publishing.cdlib.org/ucpressebooks/view?docId=ucpress>.

www.ingramcontent.com/pod-product-compliance
Lightning Source LLC
LaVergne TN
LVHW021153160826
845679LV00024B/2107
* 9 7 9 8 8 9 6 1 0 2 6 2 5 *